Why You Win or Lose

The Psychology of Speculation

Fred C. Kelly

The Turkey Story

Many years ago, I heard a story by Fred C. Kelly, the author of "Why You Win or Lose", that illustrates perfectly how the conventional investor thinks when the time comes to make a selling decision:

A little boy was walking down the road when he came upon an old man trying to catch wild turkeys. The man had a turkey trap, a crude contrivance consisting of a big box with the door hinged at the top. This door was kept open by a prop to which was tied a piece of twine leading back a hundred feet or more to the operator. A thin trail of corn scattered along a path lured turkeys to the box. Once inside the turkeys found an even more plentiful supply of corn. When enough turkeys had wandered inside the box, the old man would jerk away the prop and let the door fall shut. Having once shut the door, he couldn't open it again without going up to the box and this would scare away any turkeys lurking outside. The time to pull away the prop was when as many turkeys were inside as one could reasonably expect.
One day he had a dozen turkeys in his box. Then one sauntered out, leaving 11. "Gosh, I wish I had pulled the string when all 12 were there," said the old man. "I'll wait a minute and maybe the other one will go back."
But while he waited for the twelfth turkey to return, two more walked out on him. "I should have been satisfied with 11," the trapper said. "Just as soon as I get one more back, I'll pull the string."
But three more walked out. Still the man waited. Having once had 12 turkeys, he disliked going home with less than eight. He couldn't give up the idea that some of the original number would return. When finally only one turkey was left in the trap, he said, "I'll wait until he walks out or another goes in, and then I'll quit." The solitary turkey went to join the others, and the man returned empty-handed.
The analogy to the psychology of the normal investor is amazingly close. They hope more turkeys will return to the box when they should fear that all will walk out and they'll be left with nothing.

From: How to Make Money in Stocks by William J. O'Neil

Now you havein your hand this valuable book on investment: Why You Win or Lose by Fred C. Kelly, written in a direct and easy to understand style, identifies the four great enemies to investment success, and share his secrets as a highly successful speculator towards making money as a speculator.

CONTENTS

ACKNOWLEDGMENT

THE author acknowledges his great indebtedness to various students of the market who have contributed valuable suggestions and information for this book—especially to Colonel Leonard P. Ayres, Sullivan Burgess, Dr. Robert C. Effinger, James A. Fayne, Forrest Graves, Grace Kerr Hughes, James Hughes, Glenn Munn and O. B. Van Zant. Thanks are due to the *Cosmopolitan Magazine* and *The American Mercury* for permission to reprint material; and to Karla Weber for research as well as for an exceptionally painstaking job of typing the entire manuscript.

FOREWORD

FRED C. KELLY, amateur psychologist, writer, traveler, breeder of dogs, all-around student of human nature, has made important observations on the average human being's behavior when buying and selling stocks.

Stock market behavior of man is just as deserving of study as are the eating, drinking and sex habits of animals—the kind of studies now so popular in our psychological laboratories. The ticker tape of stock market transactions is just as good a scientific record of behavior as is the smoked drum record we use in the laboratories. The way a man behaves when buying or selling stocks gives very definite cues as to his general make-up. Moreover, the mistakes an average person has made in the past are a guide to the dangers that beset him in future. Again, such a study is important because nearly everybody is in the market. Buying and selling stocks have become a part of our general play behavior. The stock market takes the place of the bull fight of Spain, the gladiatorial combats of ancient Rome, the jousts of Merrie England. We have no other national game. One group is interested in baseball, the college bred in football, the rich in polo and yachting; but not until Mr. Coolidge's busy boom began some nine years ago did we have a game that was played by everybody, rich, poor, idler and worker, alike.

This national game had a bad set-back, but the public, I feel sure, is quite ready to attend the Wall Street Stadium the moment the next big bout is announced. Gambling has become a fixed part of our life. Nobody in America enjoys much leisure. Everybody is working at his or her job almost all day. Nine-tenths of the stuff we do is routine. Sex is so free and abundant that it hardly comes any more into the realm of excitement. Card playing has gone out among men—I don't know how long it has been since I have seen a good poker or crap game. We all get bored. Stock gambling is about the only thing that offers the same kind of thrill that big game hunting does, and you can play the market right at your desk. Call up your broker in the morning, buy a few hundred shares without moving from your seat, and the great adventure is on. It will take more than a temporary panic to weed all this out of our system and to make us content with the humdrum of the day's work.

Fred C. Kelly is the logical man to make such a study as this. Besides being a successful speculator himself he has been a keen student of behavior, both human and animal, for many years. You may find him one day watching his dog, the next his friend's child, and the next the crowd at a fire or in a broker's office. Such observations have made him wise, especially to the frailties in human nature.

There is an amazing lot of good material in his book,— really helpful material. It should be read by every one who thinks of investing or speculating in stocks. It ought to help some of us to make money. It will certainly help us to *save* money. For throughout, the book throws its weight on the side of conservatism. It is written in the extremely simple, direct, charming style that only a real craftsman can achieve with his pen.

JOHN B. WATSON.

856 Fifth Avenue
New York City

CHAPTER I

MY ADVENTURE IN TOPSY-TURVY LAND

For several years now, including much of 1929, I have had the astounding experience of being in the stock market most of the time without losing anything. Indeed, I even *made* a little. I have journeyed through the enemy's country at their expense. It would have been a wonderful adventure even if I had lost, for I had opportunity to learn of quirks and foibles of human nature in the greatest human laboratory on earth. It was like going to college, tuition free, with an occasional bonus for encouragement. Whenever the Wall Street boys have given me back a little more than I entrusted to them, I think it was because, having an insatiable curiosity about what human beings are likely to do, I have looked at the stock market in terms of crowd behavior.

In the pages that follow, I am going to try to tell what appear to be the mental hazards that make most people lose. I even hope to show just how it should be possible to take a profit from Wall Street. For the benefit of impatient readers, there is no harm in saying right now that I believe the way to win is to do exactly the opposite from what nearly everybody else is doing. In other words, one must be *contrary!*

Yet I know, simple as this formula seems, few will ever follow it. Indeed, if many followed it, then it wouldn't work. If everybody tried to buy when prices are low, then bargains would never exist. A few find bargains only because the majority never recognize bargains. The crowd always loses

1

because the crowd is always wrong. It is wrong because it behaves normally. Every natural human impulse seems to be a foe to success in stocks. And that is why success is so difficult. If you think it is easy to do invariably the opposite of what seems to be the sensible thing that everybody else is doing, just try it. At every step, one is tempted to do that which seems logical, but which is nevertheless unwise. But of all this, more later.

Looking back on my first ventures in the market, I marvel that such a greenhorn as I was ever dared to step in at all. What a lot I didn't know! I never even suspected that good news about a stock is likely to lower its price. Neither did I know that bad news may force prices upward. I had not yet found out definite reasons why men dabbling in stocks are far more likely to lose than to win. The important part played by vanity in stock losses was still a sealed book to me. Little did I suppose that the danger of losing is greatest on Monday. Neither did I understand why men are inclined to sell their good securities and keep poor ones. When I saw prices at the lowest point for the day around one o'clock in the afternoon I supposed this was mere chance.

I learned that men win or lose not so much because of economic conditions as because of human psychology. Certain mental traits that we nearly all have are barriers to success. Why, when I had a profit on a certain stock, didn't I sell it? Why did I stand by and see my profit reduced as prices went lower and lower without ever offering to sell?

It dawned on me that my behavior was almost exactly the same as that of an old man I knew in boyhood. He had a turkey trap, a crude contrivance consisting of a big box with the door hinged at the top. This door was kept open by a prop to which was tied a piece of twine leading back a hundred feet or more to the operator. A thin trail of corn scattered along a path lured turkeys to the box. Once inside they found an even more plentiful supply of corn. When enough turkeys had wandered inside the box, my friend would jerk away the prop and let the door fall shut.

Having once shut the door, he couldn't open it again without going up to the box and this would scare away any turkeys lurking outside. The time to pull away the prop was when as many turkeys were inside as one could reasonably expect.

I remember going out with the old man one day and seeing a dozen turkeys in his box. Then one sauntered out, leaving eleven.

"Gosh, I wish I had pulled the string when all twelve were there," said the old man. "I'll wait a minute and maybe the other one will go back."

But while he waited for the twelfth turkey to return, two more walked out on him.

"I should have been satisfied with eleven," the trapper said. "Just as soon as I get one more back I'll pull the string."

But three more walked out. Still the man waited. Having once had twelve turkeys, he disliked going home with less than eight. He couldn't give up the idea that some of the original number would return. When finally only one turkey was left in the trap, he said:

"I'll wait until he walks out or another goes in, and then I'll quit."

The solitary turkey went to join the others and the man returned empty-handed.

I think the analogy to the stock market is close. When I had seen a stock go to $80 a share, I was reluctant to sell at $78. By the time it had sunk to $75, I would gladly have taken $77. When obliged to let go at $65, I wondered what had ever induced me to wait so long.

I first became interested in the stock market partly because of a lurking natural disrelish for arduous toil; also, because my curiosity was piqued by the fact that nearly everything anybody chanced to tell me about stocks turned out, in the light of later events, to be almost incredibly wrong.

While following my trade as a writing man, I was exposed, as nearly everybody is, to tips on the market.

Few of these predictions seemed to come true and I wondered why nearly every man I knew should be so crammed with misinformation. To satisfy my curiosity, I began to write down secretly in a little note-book all the stock tips I heard presumably intelligent people discussing. If a friend said to buy United States Steel for a quick move, down went his suggestion in the little book. Months later I looked over the notes thus collected to see how the advance information tallied with what actually had happened. Thus I confirmed my suspicions that most of what one hears about stocks is untrue. Even after disregarding information from irresponsible people, or those who seemed unlikely to know what they were talking about, if I had bought ten shares of each stock I was advised to buy, I would have lost heavily.

Finding that the stocks people expected to go up almost invariably went down, I began to study the market to try to find out *why*. Was it because people were inclined to buy poor stocks or because they merely bought good stocks at the wrong time? I convinced myself that it was good stocks bought at the wrong time far more often than hopelessly poor stocks. To my astonishment, I learned that it is almost as easy to lose money on good stocks as on poor.

For a long time I studied market trends, business cycles, industrial conditions, reactions, rallies, various causes and effects. I learned that it is of no value to know that a stock is comparatively cheap unless one knows also whether it is cheap on the way *up* or on the way *down*. As Col. Leonard P. Ayres expresses it: "The man who buys a stock solely because of its seemingly bargain price is like a farmer with a thermometer but no almanac who thinks a hot day in autumn must be time to plant spring crops."

I discovered, also, that stocks are a little like weather. If you're experiencing the hottest day in several years, you may cheer up over the thought that it will surely be cooler tomorrow. Likewise when stocks are unusually high they are almost certain to drop.

These studies interested me more and more. I began to

make imaginary transactions in the market and carefully recorded them in my note-book. When information about a certain stock and market conditions seemed to warrant, I bought; then if the stock advanced to a point where the price seemed high enough, I sold. I also sold if the stock turned sour and seemed destined to keep on going down rather than up.

Since I had no psychological handicap of fear, no danger of exhausting limited capital in such paper transactions, I had an advantage over the fellow who plays with real money. I realized that it is one thing to be able to hit a target right in the bull's-eye, but quite another thing to do so if several men are shooting at you. (In due course I was to learn that a person carrying stocks on margin is himself a target—*always under fire*.) Yet notwithstanding my advantage of safety, I regularly lost.

Whenever I lost, I tried to find out the reason and to make capital of my mistakes. After a few weeks or months, during which I must have been a terrible nuisance to my friends by asking so many questions about the market, I did succeed in limiting losses from my hypothetical operations. One month I had a net profit of more than $200. The following month also showed a profit. Evidently I was beginning to learn how the trick was done. But born of Scotch ancestry, with a decided reluctance to engage in losing ventures, I continued to confine my buying and selling to my note-book. Finally, at the end of a year, I was astonished to observe how much I had made theoretically from my little solitaire game of make-believe. True, it was only on paper, but I had been beating the market.

As a result of such experience, I gradually acquired a willingness to buy stocks with actual money. I drew from the bank a small but neat roll of my modest, hard-wrung savings, and had a friend introduce me to a broker. It was with hang-dog air I went to the broker's office. The minute I was inside the door I glanced about furtively, fearing I might see somebody I knew. I couldn't have felt any more sneaking if the place had been a negro honky-tonk. It seemed to me that everybody was secretly saying: "Another sucker has just arrived."

The broker courteously explained to me how one buys on margin. Having stock on a margin, I gathered, is a little like having a home subject to a big mortgage, but with this important difference: When real-estate values are temporarily low one is not asked to put up more money to protect the man who holds the mortgage against you; but with stocks one is compelled to give the broker a little more margin money whenever prices fall.

Having bought a list of stocks, I picked up the paper that evening fully expecting to find either that the entire list had dropped enough to wipe out my margin, or that my broker's firm had suddenly gone into bankruptcy. Instead, I found that I already had a profit of nearly $300. "Gracious," I thought, "how ridiculous for me to have engaged all these years in honest toil! How long has this been going on!"

The next day, I didn't wait for the newspaper to give the day's fluctuations but called up my broker every few minutes. I was already discovering how difficult it is to have stocks on margin and think of anything else.

Ever since that first contact with brokers,[1] I have somehow muddled through with more profits than losses. If my losses had been heavier I should have had to quit thinking about the market and if my profits had been greater I might have become too sure of myself and quit trying to learn. Hence, I often try to reconcile myself to only modest profits

---

[1]One of the pleasant surprises in connection with my market operations is the seeming honesty of brokers. I was brought up to believe that stock brokers were unscrupulous. But after several years of dealing with them, I have yet to have a transaction in which my broker hasn't given me the benefit of any doubt. Many times I have had a broker call my attention to errors in my favor that I would never have discovered. How wrong most popular conceptions are! Most people, I presume, have an idea that the average farmer, for example, is an honest soul and that a stock broker is inclined to be a scoundrel. But after years of rather intimate relations with both farmers and brokers, if I had to go far away and leave my purse with a broker or a farmer, I would choose the broker without a moment's hesitation.

with the thought that I have at least had a valuable education at Wall Street's expense.

In the course of my several years' observations, I have discovered a long list of market blunders that nearly every one commits—blunders that may almost be considered normal crowd behavior. The Lord knows that I have made, and still make, my share. In the following chapters, I am going to review some of the commonest mistakes made by myself and others, just by way of pointing out what an average person is most likely to do.

Summing it up in advance, a brief outline of the average man's behavior in a good advancing market, with ample opportunity for profits, is something like this: Buys timidly at first, very little, if any, at low prices, but gains confidence as advance continues and buys more. He takes small profits, but noting that stocks still advance, he is sorry he sold and buys same stocks back higher up. This time he determines to get more profits, but waits too long to sell, and sees prices decline. Then he mistakes each lower price for a bargain and buys more to average up. Later, when financial pages of newspapers are full of discouragement and stocks have touched bottom, he gets scared and sells entire holdings for less than lowest price he paid. And remember that for each transaction he must contribute a fee to the kitty! Brokers' commissions are more than a million dollars a day. Small wonder that one may lose even when the market is headed upward.

Chapter II

How Our Vanity Makes Us Lose

Vanity, one's own personal vanity, is probably the greatest single enemy to stock market success. It is vanity that leads us to take small profits but large losses. Even a fraction of a point profit is all right, because, small as it is, you have nevertheless beaten the game, and this is a sop to vanity. But a fractional loss hurts your pride and instead of accepting this small loss after a stock begins to look sour, you say you'll wait until you get out even. To take a loss is a confession that your original judgment was wrong and that is not a nice thing to admit. You hate to have your broker know that you were a victim. Worse, you shrink from having yourself know it. Unconsciously, a man often says to himself: "I'm going to make up that $100 loss if it costs me $1,000!" While you are waiting to get out even, the price sinks to a point where the facts are too painful to face. You don't sell then until your broker orders you to sell.

Look into any broker's office and you may see a number of men sitting about, calm and collected, with their feet on chairs. These probably have losses to which they have long become accustomed. They are still hoping to appease vanity by getting out even and are prepared to wait. On the other hand, if you see a nervous, fidgety man, evidently not quite sure what to do, he is probably trying to make up his mind to sell and thus cinch a small profit before his vanity is in jeopardy.

Brokers, in going over their books, sometimes observe that of all completed transactions more show a profit than a loss. Yet, paradoxically, the total losses vastly exceed the profits—simply because nearly every loss is large while every profit is small. In other words, the tendency is to take small profits but let losses run.

Because of vanity, men hate to be *compelled* to do anything. We hate to concede that even a panic can make us sell stocks that we hadn't planned to sell. Hence men mortgage their homes to raise more money to give to the broker, when swallowing pride a little sooner and taking a small loss would have avoided most of the trouble.

It is vanity that makes men sell good stocks and keep poor ones in time of distress. They won't sell the poor ones, because these represent a loss; but they dispose of the gilt-edged things which still show a profit, the very ones which would eventually make up the losses. Of this we shall say more in a later chapter.

It is vanity which makes nine people out of ten, in a declining market, persistently buy *more* of the same identical stock in which they took a licking. Your friends who lost their homes by holding Chrysler which went from 135 down to 26 didn't lose so much on what they bought at first as on what they bought later to even up. Instead of quitting a stock which seems to prefer to go down and climbing aboard one which shows resistance to the decline, they say to themselves: "I'll teach that stock a thing or two; it needn't think it can throw *me* for a loss." The weaker the stock is, the more they buy as it slides downward. They return to kiss the hand that struck them.

Usually it is far safer to average upward than downward. I have found it to be a wise rule, in ordinary times, never to buy more of a stock until the original purchase shows a profit. After it has confirmed my belief that it would go up by actually doing so may be time enough to get a little more. The beauty of averaging on the way up—providing you keep within bounds—is that you are buying with profits—using the other fellow's money instead of your own. But even though you have a profit, your vanity is hurt somewhat by the knowledge that you didn't do all your buying at the bottom.

It must be vanity which makes a man carry stocks on margin—since by that method he can buy 100 shares when he can really afford to buy only 30 shares.

Perhaps it is vanity which makes a man believe all the stories put out for public consumption by professional stock market pools. Every one likes to be *on the inside,* behind the scenes, and when he hears a story, in strict confidence, that his pet stock, now selling at 80, is going to 150, because of a certain merger in the offing, he believes the story. Pools must always make the public believe that a stock will sell much higher, else they couldn't force it to the more modest price that is their real goal. Except for vanity, men wouldn't believe so much supposed inside information. They would know that the whole success of stock market manipulation must depend on secrecy. The greater a man's vanity, the surer he is of his shrewdness in picking up inside information, and hence he is just that much more likely to hang on longer and lose more.

The more thoroughly he believes in his supposed inside knowledge, the more he will risk. If he loses at first, he risks still more, expecting that certain secret plans he has heard about will soon bring a turn in his favor.

Even if the plans concerning which he had intimate knowledge were sound, they may have gone awry—since the best laid plans of mice and men sometimes do. But the speculator whose vanity gives him sublime faith in something he has heard does not use his reasoning powers; at least not until his money is all gone.

CHAPTER III

HIGH COSTS OF GREED

Next to vanity, I suppose the worst foe to good judgment that a person in the market must guard against, is old Uncle Greed. If I had only sold every stock I ever had at the price I expected to receive at the time I bought it, I should be far better off. Many a time I have placed a selling order on the same day I bought, and then—when the stock had about reached my price, cancelled the order—because I decided that a few hundred dollars profit wasn't nearly enough. And without a single exception, every time I have thus cancelled a selling order placed before my greed got to working on me, the stock later went down and I sold it below the figure I had at first planned to take.

Sad words are these—oh, if I had only sold when—! But we all use them. Because we all have our human share of greed, it is always harder to make up one's mind to sell than to buy. Every broker knows that not one-tenth as many customers will take warning and get *out* of a dangerous market, when urged to by some one in whom they have faith, as would take the same man's advice on the buying side. The explanation is that you buy because you see a chance to make money; but when you sell out you abandon present hope of further gain. Nobody likes to place himself in such a position as that, does he? Thus it appears that greed is a more potent influence than danger. People are so optimistic by nature that they are not easily scared—not easily enough for their own good. Beautiful as is optimism, we must beware of it. Not every optimist is a sucker; but most

11

suckers seem to be optimists. The optimist always thinks the market is going to move upward soon. He cannot imagine a long period of declining prices. However, once fear *has* been induced it works more quickly than does enthusiasm. Consequently stock prices *go down much faster than they go up!* Bear markets never last nearly as long as bull markets.

Maybe one reason why brokers' market letters favor buying twice as often as they do selling is not merely because brokers are by nature optimistic, and often wrong, but because customers *want* such advice. Their greed makes them eager to be told to buy.

Let a stock market forecaster predict an advance that doesn't come and the public will forgive him, but if he turns bearish too soon and warns of a slump long before it comes, his reputation is ruined. Greedy people who sold on his advice before the peak was reached will never forget about the money they think they might have made.

Not long ago a young woman asked me how to invest $1,000.

"Invest it in a trip to Europe," I told her, "for no broker can take that from you. But if you invest it while the market is so high, you will lose it all." And lose it is exactly what she did. She craved the trip to Europe, but her greed made her try to eat her cake and have it.

Here I am reminded of a telephone conversation, one end of which I overheard in a broker's office. A comely young woman was talking, evidently to a man friend who was her mentor in market transactions.

"But if it's only good for nine points," I heard her say, "maybe I'd better buy something else. You see I *must* have twenty-five points to give me the money I need before I go away."

One of the keenest men in Wall Street told me that there are seldom more than two or three times in any one year when one should buy stocks.

"Of course, I wouldn't dare be quoted on this," he said, "because I work for a brokerage house and I would lose my job. But it wouldn't hurt our business no matter how often

I published such good advice, *because nobody would believe it.*" Few can sit back and wait for bargains. Greed is an enemy of patience.

Once I asked a broker as we stood looking at the crowd of perhaps one hundred customers in his place:

"How many of these will get out of the market with a profit?"

"Nine out of ten will lose," was his candid reply, "because the first big sag in the market, even though only temporary, will wipe them out. No matter how conservative they are at first, carefully keeping reserve funds in the bank, their greed will soon lead them to have all available money up on margin and then they can't weather even a momentary reaction."

The worst losses in the market come naturally from buying stocks when they are too high-priced. And the surprising fact is that people actually buy stocks knowing full well that they are over-priced—but expecting to re-sell them at a price even higher to somebody else. That was what happened in Florida. Men who paid $10,000 for swamp land expected to pass it on to victims still more gullible than themselves.

My friend, Willard Kiplinger, well-known savant of Washington, gave me an extemporaneous explanation of how fictitious stock values, forced up by greed, must collapse. He and I and another friend were having dinner together when Kiplinger remarked:

"I suppose the stock market is like this: Here I have a dish of ice cream that cost me ten cents. Robert, the waiter, comes in and says the ice cream is all gone and no more is to be had tonight. My ice cream suddenly seems more valuable to you and you offer me, say, twelve cents for it. Then Bill, who had intended to order ice cream, makes you an offer of thirteen cents. You, being Scotch, can't resist taking a profit. Bill brags so much about the ice cream that I decide I was foolish to let it go in the first place and buy it back for fourteen cents. About that time I discover, to my dismay, that the ice cream has melted."

CHAPTER IV

PERILS OF THE WILL TO BELIEVE

After vanity and greed, perhaps the most malign influence to one trying to make money from the market is the Will To Believe. We think to be true whatever we *hope* is true. When a reputable doctor tells a man he has an incurable disease, the man is then quite likely to fall into the hands of a quack who says *he* can cure him. The patient wouldn't believe the quack ordinarily, but now if he doesn't believe his only hope in life is gone. Poor, pathetic sufferers who flock to the grave of a dead priest, expecting somehow to be benefited, wouldn't have such faith if they weren't desperately in need of it, having vainly tried everything else. Likewise, men pin their faith to poor stocks and expect these to advance 40 or 50 points, because here is their last hope of financial salvation. When a man declares confidently that a certain stock is going to advance, what he means is: "Oh, if it only *would!*" What sounds like an opinion, based on inside knowledge, is simply a hope, expressed from time to time, to bolster up one's courage.

I have seen men earnestly listening to the advice of a broker's colored porter—because he was telling what they earnestly desired to think was true. The studious fellows who work over pages of figures in the backrooms of big brokerage houses, could often give valuable advice, well mixed with caution. But customers seldom take the trouble to hunt them up, for they would rather listen to the chatty floor-men of charming personality who have little time for study but are sure that almost any stock is about to go up.

14

They are prepared to tell what customers most wish to hear. I know just one man who saw the October panic coming and when he told his employers about it, what do you suppose they did? Discharged him! His story seemed too unpleasant to be true and they decided that he must be hopelessly unreliable.

A friend of mine made a small fortune in the last big bull market only to lose it, and along with it the savings of a lifetime. He at one time had a profit of about $20,000. In his imagination he had already spent the money, building a new home, buying a new car and sending his mother-in-law on a tour which would keep her away at least six months. One morning he discovered that instead of having $20,000, his profits had shrunk to $16,000. Now, even $16,000 dropped into one's lap out of the stock market is not to be sneezed at; but once having mentally spent his $20,000, he did not like the idea of slipping back to a mere $16,000. He said to himself, "Oh, well, the drop is only temporary. When it comes back I'll again have my $20,000. To be sure of this I'll buy more stock and then only a small advance will give me my original profit."

But instead of advancing again, prices continued to drop. He now found that he must have far more stock than before to gain $20,000 profit on an average upturn of only one or two points. That $20,000, though only on paper, had become as real to him as if it were in his pocket; and his imaginary expenditures, particularly those for pleasure, had become so much a part of his scheme of life that he thought he simply *had* to have that money. So he bought still more stock. The fact that prices had been dropping should have been indication enough that the peak had been reached and that the toboggan had started down the other side. But his paper profit had obscured his vision. His profits dwindled to a mere $2,000. Somebody suggested to him that instead of waiting for two or three points' gain in the next upward rally, he should buy a certain stock about to advance twenty-five points. In other words, he was lured into buying a highly speculative stock that could move downward as easily as upward. Ready to grab at straws, he quickly lost nearly all the money he had. Toward the last he believed any silly story he heard and he was lucky to get out of the market with the clothes on his back. He was a victim of the *Will To Believe.*

CHAPTER V

WHERE BEING ILLOGICAL IS WISDOM

One of the first things I discovered about the stock market is that wrong behavior is almost sure to be seemingly logical behavior.

Indeed, one of the most charming things about the stock market is that one may prosper there by being illogical. Or at any rate, one's chances for success are greatly enhanced by doing what *seems* to be illogical. To follow mere obvious, surface logic is fatal.

Indeed, to monkey with the stock market at all is perhaps illogical, in view of all the stories one has heard since childhood about the foolhardiness of attempting to beat an unbeatable game. More, speculation is generally regarded as not only dangerous, but also as downright wicked. Profits derived from it are ill-gotten gains, because they were not won by the sweat of one's brow. Nevertheless, every conservative, successful manufacturer is a speculator. He has to be. If he doesn't buy raw materials when they're cheap—when the market is advantageous—at least part of the time, he'll finally go bankrupt. No matter how clever a salesman or advertiser a man may be, he can't withstand the odds against him if he always buys at top prices and sells his finished product in a falling market. Even buying a home is speculative. Nobody would care to have a house on ground likely to drop in value.

Maybe the very difficulty of speculation is what has brought it into disrepute. Most men who enter business eventually fail because of their inability to be successful

17

buyers and sellers. Likewise most men who speculate in stocks lose all the money they risk. Naturally, men who have failed in such an enterprise—and they are in the majority—do not speak any too highly of it. But neither do those who have been unable to master golf mention the game in terms of the highest praise. The fact remains that an occasional man speculates in the stock market as his sole means of livelihood, and contrives to do it year after year. He may not become a multi-millionaire; if he did, he would no longer have to bother with speculation. But neither does he go broke, for in that event he couldn't speculate.

The few who contrive to take more out of the stock market than they put into it do so by going contrary to what would be generally accepted as logic. They do the opposite to what the majority of seemingly intelligent speculators are doing. As an example of how the market discourages logical thinking I may note the tendency of stock prices to go down on good news and up on bad news. If you are holding a block of stock in a certain company and learn that the board of directors has decided to increase the annual dividend, you may be expected to feel pleased. You may even slap your thigh and say to yourself: "Now then, the dear old stock will advance. I'll pick up a dandy profit in the next few days."

But instead of advancing, the stock is almost certain to sell off on the good news. The market nearly always anticipates forthcoming events. Many professional stock operators will reason that there is no use keeping it any longer, because the thing they have been hoping for and which the stock itself has anticipated by a gradual increase in price, has now happened. Since there are suddenly more sellers than buyers, the first move of the stock, when the good news becomes public, is downward. On the other hand, the price may go up on bad news, because influential people think to themselves: "The worst has now happened. The stock will never be so cheap again. Let's buy it."

The most logical thing a market speculator can do,

indeed, and the thing he is most likely to do, is to buy when prices are high, and sell when prices have dropped, thus suffering a loss. Unwise as this is, it is nevertheless logical, because when stock prices are highest all the information drummed into one's ears is favorable, indicating that soon they will be still higher. But when prices are at their lowest ebb, all that one learns from the newspapers or from conversation with knowing friends is discouraging. To a mind that works logically, it is obvious that the worst is to come, and that the end of the downward swing is not yet. No wonder that ninety-seven men out of a hundred, according to brokers' records, buy at the top and sell at the bottom.

Under such circumstances, not only will you buy toward the top, but you are likely to buy at the *exact* top. Well, why not! Never was there so much good news about a stock as on the day that it reached its record high price. It was this good news which made it go there and it was the same alluring tidings which induced buying by everybody else subject to such blandishments. Every evening you discovered that if you had bought a certain stock in the morning you would have had a nice profit when the Stock Exchange closed at 3 o'clock in the afternoon. Having a logical mind you say to yourself: "The thing to do is buy tomorrow and catch the rise from now on."

Anybody knows that when a thing has happened over and over again the presumption is in favor of its continuing to happen in the same way. (Stage magicians recognize this trait of human nature and make capital of it. You have seen a magician throw balls into the air, one after another, until finally the last ball that he throws mysteriously disappears—only, he didn't throw the last one at all, but just made the motion of throwing it. Most of the audience are sure to think he really threw it—because that was what he had *been* doing.) It is this disposition to expect a stock to continue in the same direction that it has been going which leads people to buy at top prices after several days' rise, or to sell after several days of decline. Because you have thus arrived at a logical conclusion, on the very day that you decide to buy the stock goes not up but down.

We are inclined to think it a strange coincidence that immediately after we bought, our stock ceased to go up, and, that it quit going down after we sold. But this is simply because human nature in different individuals is so much alike and can stand just so much strain. The same influence that makes one person finally yield to buying or selling pressure makes nearly everybody else do the same thing. You are likely to pay the last fraction of the top figure, for the simple reason that you are an *average* person. At least, it is fair to assume that you are average. So many are!

Naturally, when all who can, be induced to buy have bought, and there are no longer more buyers than sellers, the only way the stock can move is downward.

But if you have a logical mind, you do not get excited as your stock drops. Looking back, you now realize that its price could not have kept advancing forever without going beyond its worth, and that it is now natural enough that it should drop. The setback, you figure, is probably only temporary. But each day thereafter, let us say, it takes a further violent drop. After it does this for a week or ten days you repeat the logical reasoning you followed when it was advancing. You now decide that it is likely to continue dropping indefinitely. But the day you sell is reasonably certain to mark the end of the decline, because *you are not the only one* who was finally scared into selling. You, being an average man, were merely representative. Everybody else has also sold. There being no more to sell, the stock can go no farther down.

Psychologists know that nearly all members of the human race are influenced somewhat by the day of the week. Men do not feel the same toward the world on Monday as they do on Wednesday or Saturday, and this even affects their attitude toward buying and selling securities. That being true, wouldn't Monday be the logical day for the majority of people to buy stocks? They have been to church the day before and received a spiritual comfort which has created in them a happy, optimistic frame of mind. Moreover, since Monday is the first day of a new business week, everybody else is starting off with high hopes. If you buy on Monday, you have your stocks all ready to share in the advance as the week gains momentum. What then could be more natural than for most people inclined to buy stocks at all to do so on that day? But you are a bit more shrewd than the crowd, and so you ask yourself if it wouldn't be the cagey move to *sell* your stocks on Monday, when everybody else is buying and bidding up prices.

Nevertheless, despite the seemingly unassailable logic of outwitting the crowd by selling your stocks on Monday, the cold fact is that Monday is the worst day of the week, in the long run, for selling and the best day for buying. In an advancing market you are likely to find bargains on Monday. A statistical study, covering a period of three years, showed that average prices of the so-called Dow-Jones list of stocks advanced on 71 Mondays a total of only $40 but they declined on 77 Mondays a total of $74. Putting it in another way, the average advance for a representative list of stocks over a long stretch of Mondays was only 56 cents a day, but the average Monday decline was 96 cents.[1] Moreover, declines came *more often* on Monday than on any other day. The worst days of the Big Crash of 1929 were a Tuesday in October and a Wednesday in November; but the low prices on each of these days were the culmination of selling that began and gathered momentum on the previous Monday.

Men who have been to church on Sunday—and people inclined to speculate or gamble usually *do* attend church, because they believe in every scheme for bringing good luck—probably heard there more gloom than good cheer. Departing from logic and looking the facts in the face, one remembers that preachers, picturing the terrors of the

---

[1] Incidentally, this same statistical study indicated that the smallest variations up or down in prices are likely to be on Saturdays.

hereafter, usually fill their customers with far more grim foreboding than elation. In other words, they try to round up sinners by fear more often than by hope. Moreover, it is on Sunday, when a speculator is home from the office, that his wife has a chance at him. When she sees him staring gloomily at the stock page, with a what's-the-use expression on his features, she is apt to exclaim: "Elmer, I want you to get shet of those stocks tomorrow and quit worrying about them!" Or there is a letter from Bill and Mary at college telling him they have to have more money. Mother reminds him she needs a new fur coat or the furnace has to be replaced.

Elmer, on his way to the office on Monday, wonders how in the world he is going to meet all these demands.

"Sell some stock," is the answer.

The result is that stocks tend to decline on Mondays, even though logic demands that they do nothing of the sort.

When you think the time has come to sell part of your securities, the obviously logical thing to do is to dispose of those that have risen sharply in price and keep those which have not yet had a move upward. It does not take much reasoning to see that the ones which have advanced most are probably perilously high, while those which have stood still are less likely to drop. Hence, if you sell the ones in which you have a profit and keep the others, when the tardy ones advance you will then have a profit on all.

The only trouble with this reasoning is that, though logical, it is often wrong. The stocks which advanced in price probably did so because of their merit, because of expanding business in the corporation they represent. They are therefore the ones most likely to keep on advancing. Likewise, those that stood still did so because they were already priced high enough. Especially in a time of forced selling to meet margin calls, you are naturally inclined to sell gilt-edged stocks and keep poor ones. You say to yourself: "I'll sell those that will bring me more than I paid for them and hold others until they, too, show a profit." Because of your faculty for reaching logical conclusions, you have sold the stocks most capable of giving you profits, or of pulling you out of the hole, and have kept those more likely to go lower in price than upward. In the end, you discover that you are nursing a bunch of chronic invalids.

Logically enough, the inexperienced speculator with one hundred shares of stock at $15 a share thinks to himself: "Oh, well, the most I can lose is $1,500, even if it goes down to zero." But he would be in far safer position if, instead of having one hundred shares at $15, he had ten shares selling at $150. Stocks priced at $15 decline to $10 overnight far more frequently than stocks selling at $150 drop to $100 between market sessions. Aside from the fact that higher-priced stocks have more merit, (or else they wouldn't be high-priced) low-priced stocks are dangerous because especially likely to be held by people of small means, who are easily frightened and obliged to dump stocks, in time of stress, for what they can get.

Another logical conclusion is that stocks paying a good dividend are less likely to decline than those which pay only a small return. An investor would naturally hang on to that which pays him the greatest yield, wouldn't he? But during the bull market of the last several years, one may have noted that the stocks which behaved best during recessions were those which paid only small dividends. Men of large means who can afford to hold stocks for future appreciation, regardless of immediate return, who, in fact, prefer small dividends while income taxes are still high, are the only ones who cannot be scared into selling until they are good and ready.

Since all this proves that it is fatal to proceed logically, perhaps you will conclude that the shrewd thing to do is to follow the advice of others who know more about stocks than you do. Your broker must know, because he deals in stocks all the time. Stocks are his business. Yet experience has shown that to follow a broker's market letters or verbal advice is to take the road that leads to the almshouse. To begin with, a broker is rarely by nature a scientific student of stock fluctuations, but more probably only a fellow who lives by his wits and follows mere surface indications. He is usually keen-witted, besides being uniformly courteous and agreeable, and he has a gift for picking equally charming employees; but he is too close to unimportant details to grasp in a broader way what is really going on. He is often too busy studying his customers to have much time to study stocks. The average broker, if he is truthful, can tell you a harrowing tale of money he lost before learning his lesson.

I recall becoming acquainted in a New York brokerage house with two handsome young employees, of engaging personality. They were seemingly without well-defined duties, but conferred with customers and were known as customers' men. I chanced to find out that these young men had once inherited a handsome legacy and lost it speculating in the market. They were thus compelled to go to work and their broker sympathetically gave them jobs. In consequence, these men who were incapable of handling their own funds are now advising others how to make investments.

A statistician acquaintance of mine took the trouble some time ago to place himself on the mailing list of fifteen brokerage houses, and he kept careful record of the advice in their market letters over a period of years. He worked out an original system for grading this advice. If a broker mildly urged his customers to buy stocks, his grade for that day was *plus 1;* if he was more strongly on the buying side, his grade was *plus 2;* and if his advice to buy was about as strong as it could be, then his mark was *plus 3.* Likewise, his advice to sell was graded *minus 1, minus 2* and *minus 3,* according to how emphatic it was. The compiler averaged the advice for each week and later compared the averages with what actually happened. In that way he made this astounding discovery:

Whenever the average advice from the fifteen brokers was plus 1¼, or in other words, when they were half way as urgent as they could be on the buying side, nine times out of ten it was then time, not to buy, but to sell. The market was at its top. But when prices were at the bottom and everybody should have been buying, the brokers were show-ing an average grade of *minus 1½*—that is, when the mar-ket was at its worst, they were just beginning to admit that it wasn't booming. Another statistician made a similar study of a series of market letters from fifty brokers and found that over a period of years they favored the buying side two-thirds of the time. Many financial writers on news-papers have likewise told me that they could hardly hold their jobs unless they were optimistic about the market most of the time.[1]

Even if a broker were capable of arriving at sound con-clusions regarding stock movements, it is doubtful if he could actually do so, for he would be too hampered by his prejudices. He has hundreds of customers whom he hopes to see recoup losses. Many of his intimate friends are still in the market, and with losses, in consequence of taking his advice. He doesn't *dare* think the market is going down just yet.

---

[1] It is an amusing experience to review brokers' letters covering the last four months of 1929. Nearly all the leading New York daily papers con-tain each day a column of excerpts from market letters from well-known brokerage houses. By consulting files of the New York papers one can easily glance at these columns of brokers' views and determine their value in the light of later happenings. The great Coolidge bull market reached its height on September 3. In *The New York World,* morning edi-tion, of that date, in the column of brokers' comment, the first line from broker No. 1 is "We expect a strong market." Broker No. 2 says: "We are extremely optimistic as to its (the market's) future trend." All the way down, through a column and a half of such comment, optimism is the keynote. If the market should turn reactionary, use such recessions for picking up stocks. In a general way, this optimism continued in brokers' letters clear up to the time of the big smash. Then when prices had reached incredibly low levels, due to forced selling, brokers finally decided that the time had come to be cautious. On the day that saw the final outburst of compulsory liquidation, when many stocks were avail-able at prices that may not occur again in a generation, brokers were say-ing: "We should be extremely careful about making new commitments just yet."

In other words, brokers' letters in the long run simply express the crowd-mind thought: "When they're going up, they'll always go up, but when they're going down, they'll keep on going still farther down."

I once asked a prominent broker why he put out little mimeographed sheets of advice to customers when he must realize that he is quite likely to be wrong.

"Because," he frankly told me, "it is necessary, to keep business alive. Members of the human race are slow in coming to decisions, but the slight impetus they get from reading what a broker says may be enough to make them buy or sell when otherwise they would do neither."

Still, might not friendship with a good broker be a convenience? The broker is at least in a position to see what other speculators are doing and can pass out valuable and confidential information. True enough. But the danger is that if you know your broker well enough for him to tell you things in confidence, he probably knows you well enough to be in close touch with your account on his books. He knows, and you know that he knows, exactly what you are doing. Therefore if you occasionally go contrary to his advice and back your own judgment, you are almost compelled to be stubborn and stick to your mistake, if you do make a mistake; your vanity will not permit you to let him see that you know you are wrong. You must stick to the course on which you started in the conviction that it will be the right one in the long run. To do otherwise would be an admission that you are not fit for the game. You do not care to admit that— least of all to your broker. If you know him intimately, you want him to regard you as a financial wizard. Beware, then, of knowing your broker well enough to play golf with him!

I even know a man who invariably has an account in at least two different brokerage houses solely to be able to buy or sell contrary to one broker's advice without hurting that broker's feelings. "About half the time," this man reports, "when a broker whispers something to me that he thinks I should do, I know he has unconsciously been influenced by the behavior of various customers, most of them sure to be wrong, and I am inclined to do exactly the opposite—but in another office where he can't know that I have coppered his advice."

Well, if brokers can't tell you about stocks, then surely the sensible thing to do is to find somebody who can—somebody who has a proved record of successful speculation—maybe some friend who has, and is willing to impart, reliable information. But in practice even his advice may be worthless. A man capable of successful speculation presumably has enough self-respect and pride not to wish to lead others into disaster. He dares not advise them to take risks that he himself may take. I happen to know a man—know him very well—who made a considerable sum in the stock market a year or two ago, and a half dozen of his friends began to speculate on his advice. But while he himself was making money every one of them lost. Yet his intentions were the best. True, they did not lose much. He was so afraid that they might lose and place the blame on his shoulders that he advised them to buy only conservative, safe securities. In fact, they were so safe that they could not fluctuate much in either direction and therefore did not offer much profit to speculators. Consequently, they were neglected and dropped slightly in price. In other words, the price this man's friends paid for insurance against losing much was to lose a little.

Since brokers don't know much about stocks, and even successful speculators are unable to give profitable advice, then the only logical thing to do is to go to the head of a successful business enterprise for information about conditions of his own industry and the prospects of his own stock. Here, surely, one will get information from the fountain head, and it cannot well be wrong. Yet the fact is that it is almost sure to be wrong, for the man is prejudiced about his own stock just as a mother has biased opinions about her own children. Perhaps he speaks enthusiastically of stock in his own company, because in the back of his head a plan is forming for a new stock issue that will be highly profitable to himself and his associates. His self-interest compels him to think highly of the stock. But on the other hand, he may speak disparagingly of the stock's future, because he himself sold most of his holdings too soon. He wishes he could buy it back at a bargain price, and the only way he

can hope to do this is not by expressing himself in too optimistic terms, but by viewing the stock's future somewhat
gloomily. Mind you, he may be honest enough in all he says,
but his point of view is warped by his personal prejudices.
"The biggest bear is always a sold-out bull." Moreover, no
matter how truthful his statements may be, it may lead one
astray, for there is always the danger of buying his stock at
a time when the rest of the public is not in a buying mood.
Whenever there are more sellers than buyers, the price will
drop, no matter how good the stock is.

One does sometimes hear of inside tips from professional
stock operators who are nearly always successful. It might
be logical to act on such tips—save for the fact that such
information is almost sure to be wrong. At the time one is
told that a professional operator is buying on a big scale,
the chances are that he is really selling. If he were buying,
come to think of it, he wouldn't say anything about his
belief any more than a man who wanted to buy a horse
advantageously would go about telling how much he
admired it.

It begins to look, doesn't it, as if the sensible and logical
thing to do is to follow one's own judgment? But of course
one's own judgment is made up of all kinds of information,
which must be weighed and interpreted. Such information
probably includes that to be found in the newspapers. You
observe in first-page news items that stocks are having a
boom and that all signs point to higher prices. This news
has become so important that it can no longer content itself
on the financial page but has bounded to page one.
Evidently it is a logical time to buy stocks. Is it, though?
After you have bought, you learn that the stock news
reached the first page because not only the high prices, but
also the volume of buying, had been exceptional. By the
time you buy, all the other speculators have already bought.
Who, then, is going to bid for your stocks?

If stocks show a perverse tendency to decline in price the
minute you buy them, why not fool them by engaging in
what is commonly known as selling short? In other words,

why not sell stocks that you haven't yet bought, on the assumption that you can fulfil your selling contracts later by picking up the stocks at lower prices? The danger in this is that by the time you have decided to sell short, taking the bear side of the market, your move is so logical that it is equally obvious to everybody else in the market. Inasmuch as many others are now under obligation to deliver stocks sold short, everybody becomes nervous and eager to acquire such stocks. Thus a sudden demand is created, temporarily at least, for stocks that were sold only recently at falling prices. With everybody trying to buy at once, prices rise. The market has what is called a rally, and many who sold stocks that they didn't have are now compelled to buy at unfavorable prices.

Many speculators, despairing of hitting upon the one stock that will turn out the most profitable, buy a diversified list, hoping that at least one stock on it will be a real prize. But on this list there may also be one that turns out to be a very bad egg. In that event an illogical thing happens. While one good stock will not help the poor ones, a bad stock may contaminate all the rest, like one rotten apple in a barrel. When you suffer a loss on one stock, you usually try to make up the loss by holding the others—even after you have gained all the profit on them that can be reasonably expected. Instead of selling them when prices are booming, you keep them too long, and may have to throw them overboard in the end at a loss.

Another illogical thing in the stock market is the fact that the man who believes most implicitly that a certain stock is to advance, say thirty or more points, is less likely to be right than if he felt less sure. As already pointed out, the man who feels too sure is likely to be a victim of the Will To Believe.

Perhaps one of the most shocking things about the stock market to a man who thinks along logical lines is its tendency, discussed in a previous chapter, to lose his money for him even while his stocks are headed in a general way upward. Being naturally conservative and cautious, he buys timidly at first when an upward swing is getting under way, but as the market gains momentum he buys more. From time to time, as the market continues its upward trend, it suffers price reactions. These are not dangerous to a man who has only a few shares of stock, but to one who has been increasing his holdings a temporary drop of a few points may be enough to wipe out his entire capital. A little figuring will show how this may be true. If a man of small capital has ten shares of stock bought at a low price and never buys any more, a drop of one point in the price of that stock costs him only $10, but if he reinvests his profits until he has two hundred shares of various stocks, a drop of one point in the average price of those stocks will cost him $200.

One might think, logically enough, that when stocks show strength at the opening of the market in the morning, they might be expected to be strong during most of the day. Then one could buy at the opening and sell an hour or two later at a profit. But it frequently happens that about ten minutes past ten, New York time, the market takes a turn in the opposite direction from that in which it opened. This is because ten or fifteen minutes are usually required to dispose of the accumulation of buying and selling orders placed the night before. Once these are out of the way, the market behaves according to whatever the latest financial developments happen to be.

Likewise, at the noon hour, when men's energies are said to be highest of the day, and prices might be expected to be high, there is a fair chance of having the lowest prices of the day—because many floor traders go to lunch between 12 and 1 o'clock, and are likely to dispose of their stocks before they go.

Many reasons might suggest a stiffening of stock prices in midsummer when men spend time out in the open air and sunshine and might have a more cheerful outlook on life. But a study of market trends for the last twenty years shows that if you bought a diversified list of good stocks early in August and sold them late in September, or early

October, you would have a profit more often than a loss.[1] This may seem illogical until we recall that August is the vacation season. When about to go on a vacation a man doesn't care to have the stock market on his mind. Not only does he wish to be free from worry, but because he is tired and in need of rest, business prospects don't seem any too bright and he is willing to sell his stock holdings for whatever the market offers. But when he returns from his vacation a month later, rested and optimistic, he is sure that business is in for a boom and buys stocks confident of advancing prices.

One might logically expect that toward Christmas time when men are presumably filled with the idea of good will

-----

[1] The Dow-Jones averages of August 1 and September 30, for the years 1910 to 1929, inclusive, were as follows:

1910	76– 79½	1920	86– 83
1911	86– 76	1921	70– 71
1912	90– 94	1922	96– 96
1913	78– 80	1923	88– 88
1914 Market Closed		1924	105–104
1915	76– 90	1925	134–144
1916	89–103	1926	162–158
1917	92– 84	1927	185–197
1918	81– 84	1928	216–240
1919	108–111	1929	350–345

From this table one may note that the averages were up eleven years out of nineteen, down six years, and remained the same two years, from August 1 to September 30. (But in at least one of the two years when the figures were no higher after two months, there had been an intermediate time when one who bought on August 1 might have had a profit.) From these figures it appears that one has twice as good a chance for an advance as for a decline during the two months that include the most popular vacation season. Moreover, the total number of points that the averages declined from August 1 to September 30, in twenty years was only thirty-three—but in the years that they showed an advance during the same period, the total gain was 90½ points. In other words, good stocks are at least twice as likely to show a profit as a loss if bought August 1 and sold September 30. But even if there is a loss on your stocks, it will be considerably less than the profit past experience justifies you in expecting. You have better than an even chance to win.

toward one and all, and business is being stimulated by Christmas buying, the stock market should swing upward. Yet statistics show that one may usually count on a temporary slump between the 13th and 18th of December. The explanation is doubtless that people are in especial need of cash when aggressive proprietors of department stores, and other clever merchants, are bringing the most persuasion to bear for the purchase of gifts in celebration of the birth of Christ. It is an old saying that the bulls may have Thanksgiving, but the bears usually get Christmas.

I recall a thoroughly logical bit of reasoning by a friend of mine just at the close of the great debacle in November 1929. He had noticed a stock that had steadily resisted the downpour of selling and was only a few points lower than it had been before the big catastrophe occurred.

"Any stock that can do that must be extra good," he reasoned; "therefore when the turn does come, in a day or so, it will be the first stock to swing sharply upward."

He was right about the stock being good, but when the upturn finally came, that stock went down more than on any day during the decline. What probably happened was that many people who still had profits in it suddenly decided to sell it to raise cash for buying bargains. Moreover, inasmuch as the stock was indeed especially good, and showed a disinclination to go down, nobody had dared to sell it "short." Hence there was no sudden necessitous buying to give the stock an impetus back upward.

A logically minded person hardly dares trust his senses at all. Nearly everything you see proves to be untrue. On the Sunday following the fatal October Tuesday of 1929, when Wall Street was in panic, newspapers all over the country carried big first-page headlines about the flood of buying orders that would swamp the market on Monday morning. A canvass of brokerage houses in New York by newspaper men indicated that poor tired clerks would scarcely be able to handle such a downpour of buying orders from bargain hunters. Now all this buying would make the prices go up, wouldn't it? Yet prices were downward all day Monday from the sound of the opening gong until the close. Newspaper stories of buying orders had notified all wiser people who had bought a day or two previous that here would be a lovely time to sell. To be logical is dangerous, if not fatal.

When, then, is one to do? We have seen that no matter what plan one follows, the tendency is for it to be wrong. Yet we know that some people do speculate in the stock market successfully. How do they do it? What plan do they follow?

It must be evident by this time that the only safe method is to be illogical. If you are logical you merely do what everybody else is doing. You can't make money that way any more than a group of people can get ahead in the world by washing one another's clothes. You can make a profit in the market only by outwitting the majority of other people. But you can't do that if you follow the same plan that they do. In a later chapter we shall try to determine what, if anything, is the answer.

CHAPTER VI

THERE'S A POOL IN IT!

Though the chances for success of a stock market pool depend in a large measure on its secrecy, almost anybody—and particularly the man in the chair next to you at your broker's office—will volunteer to tell you exactly what a given pool is up to. Indeed, it seems doubtful if any other subject produces such vast stores of misinformation, all within easy reach of even the humblest seeker.

Besides all the undependable rumors about the actual and concrete plans of this or that pool, there is a widespread myth about a pool's miraculous powers. In the minds of amateur speculators, every pool is rarely gifted at foreordination and omniscience and has a magic wand with which it can put the price of a stock wherever it sees fit.

One speculator whispers to another the name of a stock.

"There's a *pool* in it," he says. "They're going to shove it up 30 points. Better get aboard now."

At the word pool the other speculator has pricked up his ears.

"Is it accumulating stock now?" he inquires.

"Sure. It's apt to move any day."

Maybe the truth is that the pool, if one exists, has been feeding out misinformation about a forthcoming move in that stock for the very purpose of unloading its own holdings.

Men who form and operate pools do not have 100 per cent infallibility. When they succeed in beating the market it is not always or entirely because they have inside information about a particular stock, but mainly, perhaps, because they

34

have learned by experience and observation more about crowd psychology than the general run of speculators. In other words, they are able to anticipate what thousands of others in the market are most likely to do, and to outplay them.

Shrewd pool managers long ago learned that, because man is by nature a bargain hunter, it is easy to sell him stocks when prices are declining. For this reason probably a majority of them sell their stocks to the public on the way down instead of on the way up. In other words, most of us in our zeal for bargains are poor judges of bargains. People remember a stock's former high price long after they forget that it also had a former *low* price. We may think a stock is cheap simply because the price is lower than it was yesterday, disregarding the possibility that it may be still lower tomorrow. Wise men do not buy a stock until it has been through severe tests and shown an unwillingness to go any lower. But most of us are too impatient to wait for a stock to show its mettle—and consequently we are a great help to the pools.

We see a certain stock climb from, say, $65 a share to $88. Each time it registers a little higher than it has been before we wish we had bought it sooner. As we have already seen, the human mind is inclined to assume that whatever has been happening will continue to happen. Hence we decide that a stock that has been on the up-grade will keep right on in the same direction. We are greatly assisted in this belief by rumors that the pool is planning to put it above $100 a share.

The pool has carefully contrived to have just such rumors floating about. Unless there is a widespread notion that the stock is going much higher, who will rush in to buy it?

If we believe that the stock is to sell at more than $100, naturally it looks like a real snap if it is much under its previous top price of $88. You and I and many others say: "If it drops down to $85 again, we'll buy it." So we put in what is called an open order with a broker to buy as many shares as we can afford, at $85.

These open orders to buy at a point a trifle below present price are what the pool managers dote on, for they provide a ready market for the stock they have to sell. Not only does the low price look attractive to the public, seeking bargains, but as the price declines farther, more and more people are able to buy, just as more buyers are always available for a low-priced automobile than for a more expensive one. The pool would like to sell all the stock it has at the exact top, but knowing this to be impossible, its managers don't mind feeding out shares on the way down, so long as the average price they receive is considerably above what they paid.

They may start buying at 40, with the intention of making an average of 30 points profit. To do this they may force the price momentarily to 90. But they know they can't hope to sell much stock at that figure, and are glad enough to keep on selling as the price declines until they may sell their last stock at what the public regards as a rare bargain, maybe well under 70. Meanwhile, to make their stock touch 90, they must busily spread shrewdly planned propaganda that it is sure to go to, say, $120.

When a group of men form a pool to speculate in the stock of a corporation, they like to include in their number some one who can furnish advance inside information about the company. Maybe this insider is a member of the board of directors. He knows, many weeks before the public has any chance to find out, if his company is going to report increased earnings. By the time the public hears that such good news is soon to appear, carefully directed rumors say that the pool is buying. Probably the pool has already picked up most of the stock it wants and is now buying only enough to give support—that is, to keep the price steady and thus make the stock look attractive.

One member of a well-organized pool may be a banker. Indeed, a banker comes in handy, no matter what one is trying to do in a business way. He not only knows where the money bins are and how much money is available, but is in position to peek behind the scenes and discover which other folks hold certain stocks and what they may be up to. But most important of all in each pool is the manager, the man who determines when to buy and sell and in what quantities. Whatever the manager does, if he is competent, this much is certain: he will maintain great secrecy. If anything leaks out about what the pool is doing it is usually because it suits the purpose of the pool to have such information abroad.

When we hear that a pool is about to put a stock up, it would be more accurate to say that the pool is about to have the *public* put the price up. All that the pool manager can do is to use his knowledge of crowd psychology to make the public do as he desires.

When the time is ripe for the pool to stimulate interest in its stock, it begins to advertise, just as a merchant advertises when he wishes to attract customers for a new line of goods. The pool manager employs one of the greatest advertising mediums on earth—the ticker tape. The advantage of this over ordinary newspaper advertising is that it is sure to be seen mainly by possible customers—those who watch stock price movements. It is class advertising. Moreover, once one has placed one's advertisement on the ticker tape, it is reprinted on the financial pages of newspapers, which thus provide a tremendous volume of free publicity. Of course, no advertising space is actually offered for sale on the ticker tape. It carries only the little abbreviated price quotations, such as GM 4.38%. But that is all the advertising a pool needs. Its members know that when their favorite stock begins to look active on the tape, with a decidedly upward trend in price, traders in all parts of the country will instantly observe the fact.

Sometimes, through one or more brokers' offices, they negotiate sales of this stock at slightly increasing prices. These sales are really just to each other, and represent neither profit nor loss. But credulous men who see these sales recorded on the ticker tape begin to exclaim: "Look-ee here! There's evidently something doing in General Bootlegging Preferred. It's being bought in *big lots*. Must be about to have its move." The public reasons: "Those who buy such big blocks must have inside information that a rise is coming. Let's buy now before the real rise starts." (A pool has a big advantage in the fact that the public may usually be counted on to continue making the same blunders that it has in the past.)

When the public begins to crowd one another and bid for such stock, the price naturally advances. Members of the pool now cease selling merely to each other and sell to the public. When they have disposed of their stock at prices beyond its value they walk quietly away, chuckling merrily, leaving the public to hold the sack.

What if a member of a pool himself leaks information? This sometimes happens and when it does, punishment, swift and drastic, is meted out to the one who has broken faith, and to all his followers. If he has told his friends to buy a certain stock for quick profits, then the price must be forced down, and kept down, until everybody who believed in this man's information is convinced that he was wrong. Every effort is made by the pool manager to give a sharp loss to those who expected to profit from the leak. If the member of the pool doesn't suffer a money loss, he at least becomes so thoroughly discredited in the eyes of his friends that his punishment is ample.

The question may be asked if there is any way of knowing, just from the behavior of a stock on the tape, if the present stage of a pool operation has been completed. Occasionally, the evidence is fairly plain. Whenever there is a tremendous turnover of stock—perhaps one-fifth of all the shares that exist in that particular stock—at the top of a sharp advance, one may be reasonably certain that a considerable portion of these sales are spurious, just to create a market in which to unload pool holdings. At such a time, any individual who bought that stock for speculation should promptly sell.

Amateur traders are always saying that this stock or that hasn't yet had its move, and always implying that sooner or later it just naturally must move upward. Indeed, their confidence almost suggests that there are laws, rigidly enforced, which *require* every stock on the board to sell at higher prices when its turn comes. The real explanation is that, whether in the stock market or elsewhere, we are always expecting the things to happen that we hope will happen.

Amateur traders usually buy more readily than they sell, and this isn't surprising. Since everybody is looking for profits, it is natural that people are prompt to accept the first sign of higher prices as a signal to buy. Hence the pool has comparatively little difficulty in putting up prices. It is an old saying that stocks do not *go* up but are *put* up; and this is probably true. With 1,000 different stocks on the New York Stock Exchange alone, why should anybody pick out one stock rather than another, unless it has been handled by a pool in a manner to attract attention? In other words, why should anybody pick out an unadvertised stock any more than one should buy an unadvertised soap rather than another soap that is cleverly exploited? But, I repeat, if they are put up by pools it is only because the pools are clever at a kind of silent ballyhoo intended to lure the public. The real motive power which forces higher prices is the buying by thousands of small investors and small speculators. You and I, and all the rest like us, are the ones who put prices up. Without us the pools would be helpless.

Since each pool has a manager and he is just a human being, it naturally follows that pools have individual human traits which sometimes show themselves in their methods of operation. Shrewd speculators who are close observers of pool activities sometimes declare that they can identify the manager of a pool by the way a stock behaves. Having observed how a stock has acted in the course of a previous operation under the direction of this same manager, they try to foretell what the current stock may be expected to do later on. If such deductions were dependable one would know just when to sell out ahead of the crowd.

Many clever operators play the market by means of charts which show the movements of a stock, day by day, or even hourly, over a period of many months, together with the daily volume of sales and their relation to price fluctuations. A study of such charts often indicates the support levels and accumulating levels of certain stocks.

The chart of Radio Corporation, prior to its sensational move upward of more than 100 points, would have shown an observer that the stock had twice sold above $100 a share and then sunk back to about $85 without ever going below the 85 mark. Evidently the pool was prepared to support the stock at $85 and buy all the public cared to offer at that figure.

According to the chart, Radio should have been bought at or near $85, and any one who so bought it would have doubled his money within a few weeks. But other charts showing similar support levels may only serve to lure a person into buying a stock that is soon to go much lower. A certain motor stock once had a habit of fluctuating in the 90's for several weeks. Whenever it went down to 91, it seemed to lose interest in going any lower. Many bought the stock because of the way it looked on the chart. Then a day came when it never stopped going down until it was well under 80. Later it went much lower. By that time many who had bought in the 90's became alarmed and sold out at a serious loss.

In other words, it is easier to keep a chart than to interpret its story. Even experienced chart-players confess that it is difficult to distinguish between accumulation and distribution. The pool manager may be contriving to make a stock look as if it is a good purchase for the very purpose of creating a ready market for shares the pool desires to sell.

To guess what the pool is doing by means of charts would be easy enough if the pool manager were invariably stupid, and did not know that the public is constantly trying to surmise, by graphs and whatever other means are available, what he is about to do. But, knowing that his every move is being watched, the pool manager is naturally on the alert to cover his tracks and make it appear that he is doing exactly the opposite of what he is actually doing.

As an example of how a clever pool manager may fool the

chart readers, I chance to know about an operation in a certain industrial stock. This stock had been fluctuating for some months between 115 and 125. Owners of large blocks of the stock, who frequently used it for collateral loans at the bank, would have been satisfied with a valuation of 125, but did not like to have it take dips much lower. They sought the aid of a professional pool manager. He not only succeeded in forcing the level of the stock considerably higher, but did so at almost no expense. All he did was to buy stock every time it sold below 120 and sell it every time it went much above that figure. He ran no risk in his buying orders, for the stock was really worth more than 120; and by promptly selling on only small advances, he was able to operate with only a modest amount of capital put up by the men interested. After a few weeks of this, chart observers were much impressed by the fact that the stock had "made a line" at 120. They took this to be significant. Evidently a pool was accumulating stock at 120 for a big forward move. Rumors of such a projected move began to reach brokers' offices and the public began to buy. Soon the stock reached 130, instead of the 125 that would have satisfied its sponsors, and it didn't drop below that for many months. Meanwhile, the work of the pool having been accomplished, all pool operations were discontinued. The stock was kept at a new higher level by the obliging public.

Frequently, the pool manager is able to make his stock look more desirable at the very time when he knows it has exhausted its immediate possibilities. Equally important, he can often make it look worse just before it starts to rise— when the pool itself needs a little more stock at low prices and desires to frighten timid holders into selling.

Every little while a stock makes a quick advance of from 5 to 10 points and then shortly afterward loses half of this gain. The reason is so-called profit-taking. Traders are not content to wait indefinitely for the ultimate high price they expect, but are glad to clinch a small profit while they have it, and take their chances on getting the same stock back again at a slightly lower price. If a pool considered only its final goal, and had to buy all the stock offered from time to time by others who wish to take small but quick profits, the operation might be too expensive.

If it kept right on forcing prices upward, with no temporary recessions, it would make more money for the public than for itself—which is the last thing on earth a God-fearing pool desires to do. However, pool operators sometimes purposely let the public make money in certain stocks for a time—in order to have them tell their friends of their good fortune and thus create a market for the stocks.

Knowing that others will take profits after a brisk upward move, the pool beats them to it and sells part of its own stock before an intermediate recession has been completed. Suppose that a stock has been lurking for some time at, say, $44 a share and then suddenly climbs within a few days to $55. The top price of $55 is forced solely for advertising purposes and is maintained only momentarily. For several days thereafter, perhaps, the price is $52, holding there with decided firmness. The public says:

"Oh, goody, goody! Here's a chance to get it for 52, three points below its high, and they say it's going to 80."

But as soon as the public has bought all it desires at 52, the pool quietly permits the price to recede to 48, where it may start in buying again for its own account.

Beside the profits it makes on the major up-swing in a stock, a pool aims also to gain a return from buying and selling at the right time on these minor fluctuations. Hence it is frequently necessary for it to hoodwink the public into buying or selling at the *wrong* time. When the pool has more stock than it wants, the stock must be made to look so attractive that the public will reach for it. But just before important favorable news is to appear and the pool wants more stock for a sharp advance, the public must be induced to sell part of the stock it has been patiently holding.

When little stock is in the public's hands, that stock is said to be in good technical position. But if the public is loaded up with a certain stock then wise observers say that while it may be intrinsically good its technical position is poor. "Too much stock is hanging over the market." At such a time wise speculators aim to let that stock alone. They wait until the public has tired of it and sold. Thousands of us regularly assist the pools by furnishing the capital for margin and carrying charges until such time as the pool is ready to take the stock over.

Two methods are always available for dislodging stock from the public's hands: by scaring it loose, and by wearing it loose. In other words, we may be frightened into selling when we shouldn't, due to fear of a possible loss, or we may sell simply because our patience is worn down. After holding a stock for several months in expectation of a rise which fails to come, it is natural to think: "That blamed old stock is never going to move. I'm practically even on it. I might as well sell and put my money into something that *will* move."

Pool managers have learned by experience and observation just how long human patience can hold out in a given market situation and they quietly out-wait the public. The time required to discourage those who are holding an inactive stock often runs from four to seven months—sometimes even longer. During that time, the pool in self-defense must make the stock look just as unattractive as it possibly can. Thus it happens that while many traders lose money by receiving their information too late, many others lose by having their information too soon and sell out in disgust perhaps right on the eve of a rise.

In New York is a statistical student who has enough friendships in leading brokerage offices to obtain from time to time a statement of the number of shares held on margin of a score or more of stocks in which he is usually interested. For eleven years now he has carefully tabulated the total of these lists, and by a study of them he has come to know just what may be considered a normal marginal holding of these stocks. By his observation not only of these figures but of the accompanying market performances in the past, he is able to say with confidence that when the public holding of a given stock is above a certain point—which point his experience enables him to recognize—that stock will *not* move upward.

(How I would dote on knowing intimately even one chief bookkeeper in a big brokerage house, who would quietly whisper various information to me. It would be even more helpful than appears at first thought, for what happens in one big office is almost sure to be duplicated elsewhere. It is well-nigh unheard of for the public to be doing more buying than selling of leading stocks through one broker, but more selling than buying at another place. The crowd is fairly sure to behave as a unit.)

Since it is impossible for most of us to find out from brokers' records how much of the floating supply of a stock is in public hands, I asked this statistical student if there were any short-cut method by which one could detect too heavy public holding just by looking at the newspaper reports of market transactions.

"You may at least be fairly sure of this much," he replied. "When a stock climbs briskly several points higher than it has been before and then *stays* at or near that high point, the public is sure to buy it and hold it until they finally change their minds about its being about ready to go still higher."

When the papers are full of reports about a certain industry being in a thriving condition, the public may rush in to buy stocks in that industry and such public holding is the very thing that may prevent the stocks, during several weeks or months, from fully responding to good news about the industry.

If you held a good stock for a long time, but finally grew discouraged because it wouldn't advance and sold, then the stock was almost sure to take a sudden interest in life once again and start sensationally upward. While you held on, it was just playing 'possum. The pool wasn't waiting just for *your* stock. The explanation is simply that since human nature is everywhere much the same, a normal person has just an average store of patience and hence we all behave about alike. When you and I have become wearied from holding a stock that seems hopelessly disinclined to come up to our optimistic expectations, and tell our broker to sell, it is almost certain that hundreds of other holders in the same impatient mood are likewise selling. Closing out our stocks at the wrong time is the penalty we pay for being just average.

In accumulating the stock it wants, a well-managed pool has a methodical way of bidding just so much each day and not a fraction more. If it is willing to pay $40 a share for whatever is offered, it bids exactly 40 and pays no attention to offerings at 40¼. In the language of the stock exchanges, it does not *reach* for stock. There may come a time, however, when it may suddenly and unexpectedly bid several points higher. Its method of doing so serves as a good example of how a pool manager may use his knowledge of mental processes in the human animal.

If you are seated in a broker's office, day after day, looking at the figures on a great area of blackboard representing the constantly changing prices of various stocks, or if you are looking at the quotations as they appear on the tape, you may observe some morning that a certain stock, long quiet and selling within a narrow price range, has suddenly become active. Not only active, but at sharply advancing prices. Each sale of several hundred shares is a fraction above the previous sale and after only a few minutes the stock sells four or five points higher than it did when this brisk little movement started. Then prices begin to recede once more and perhaps after half an hour the stock is quiet again. Probably the best price you can obtain, if you try to sell, is the same that has been prevailing for many days.

Here is the explanation: Mr. Pool Manager knows that the average man likes to tickle his own vanity by getting a little better price for whatever he has to sell than other people are getting. When a stock has been selling for a long time invariably around $40, a number of holders of such stock are likely to say to themselves: "I'm not going to sell at $40 but I'll take $43." Others may put their selling price at $44 or $45. They don't wait until the stock is selling at the higher figures before trying to sell, but place their selling orders in advance. These open orders may be on the brokers' books for weeks before they can be executed.

The pool manager perhaps makes it worth while for the specialist handling that particular stock on the floor of the Stock Exchange to tell him just how many open orders to sell are on his books, and at what prices. Perhaps the total number is not enough to be worth thinking about. But eventually the number will become important. Then, some fine balmy morning, the pool manager says to his broker, or brokers: "Buy all the stock that is offered between 40 and 45."

That brings about the sudden run-up, somewhat suggestive of a mouse darting out of its hole after a piece of cheese and right back into its hole again. The stock is bid up from 40 to 45, all within a few minutes, and then promptly begins to recede. If the enterprise were not quickly carried out, many who had orders in at 42 would change their minds and raise their price. The pool must clean up all open orders on the various brokers' books before the public has time to learn what is going on. A few traders, noting that the stock recently offered at 40 is now selling at 45, offer their holdings "at the market," that is, without specifying the price. But to their great disgust, the price has probably dropped two or three points by the time their orders are executed.

One may well be suspicious of a stock that makes a new high price at what appears to be the probable peak of a bull market. The chances are that this price is not based on real value of the stock itself so much as on an artificial situation created by a pool. But, on the other hand, when a stock sells higher than it ever has before, or at any rate, the highest in many months, right at the *beginning* of a bull market,— that stock will bear watching and should probably be bought. The price is much more likely to represent genuine value than at any other time. To begin with, just after a long decline, and before a new bull market has gained headway, most speculators haven't much money and pools are inactive. (You see, there's no use fooling a public that hasn't any money. It is a public saturated with profits that a pool loves to lure into unwise purchases.) When stocks are thus permitted to drift and seek their own levels, the behavior of a stock that forces its way up is significant. If it can go up without any propaganda or manipulation by sponsors, it will probably go much higher when the market is all ready for a big general advance.

Reversing the situation, when a stock of superior merit goes down gradually of its own weight, under a downpour of selling such as occurred in October and November 1929, it may be slow to come back—much slower than inferior stocks are—simply because there is no sudden short cover-ing to bring it back. Nobody sold it short for the reason that the merit of the stock and the danger of a corner in it, made this too dangerous. Some one may notice that a stock declined only ten per cent of its former price, while other stocks went down thirty per cent, and say: "It behaved so well that it must be good. Hence it will come back rapidly. I'll buy it for a quick move on the rally." But it will probably come back just as slowly and sluggishly as it went down.

Pool managers know that after a long dull period, when the time has come to force the price of a stock upward, the first few points are sure to be the hardest sledding. This is because a multitude of people who bought at slightly higher prices, and have been disappointed, are anxious to get out even and are quick to sell when their original buying price is reached. The pool must shove ahead through this heavy stratum, forced to absorb stock at every step, until a higher altitude is reached.

For an entirely different reason, it often happens, that after the first difficult ten- or twelve-point rise, a pool is able to force a stock price thirty or forty points higher with surprising ease. The explanation is that the pool is aided by all the boys who think the price is too high and start to sell the stock short. This creates an artificial but sure demand for the stock as the advance continues; for the shorts are easily alarmed and decide to buy the amount they had sold. Then, since people always prefer to buy during an advance, the brisk activity of the stock, as the shorts run to cover, invites still more buying.

Just as stocks are said not to go up so often as they are *put* up, likewise many stocks do not go down much until they are forced down by pool operation. Pool managers are quick to take advantage of any unfavorable news and to make such news seem more disastrous than it really is. A while ago, the head of a big steel company died suddenly. Though he had been nominally president of his company, he had for a year or two been comparatively inactive. Indeed, his death was in reality an immediate benefit to the company because it placed complete authority in the hands of younger and more aggressive men. But the pool began to dump stock of that company for the purpose of spreading fear and driving down the price of the stock. Other stockholders, noting the sharp decline in prices, began to offer their shares for whatever they could get. The price dropped within a few hours more than 30 points. At that low level the pool bought all the stock offered and then let the news leak out through its publicity channels that the death of the steel man hadn't been so harmful to his company after all.

Because an extremely low price is thus forced by pool manipulation, and is part of a plan to acquire, cheaply, block of stock expected to sell higher, many observers are inclined to follow this rule:

When a stock drops sharply and actively to the lowest price in a long time, but during three months thereafter fails to go still lower, then it is probably going, not lower, but higher.

Pool managers even reckon with such human factors as people's number habits. Most of us unconsciously have definite number habits that enter into our thinking processes. Ask almost anybody suddenly to write down a number between one and ten and the chances are two out of three that he will write seven. For some unknown reason seven is a favorite number with a majority of us. Likewise numbers ending in either five or zero are handy numbers. Our preference for them probably goes back to the days when we were learning the multiplication table and found that we could use multiples of five much more rapidly than other numbers.

According to the census figures, there are always more people aged thirty-five than either thirty-four or thirty-six, simply because it is so easy to say thirty-five to the census man for any age near that figure. Judges sentence many men to ten years in the penitentiary but few to nine years. Even wage scales show the influence of number habits. A man seldom receives $26 a week, but he often receives $25 or $30, or $27.50, which is a compromise between two multiples of five.

Now, these same number habits naturally are felt in stock transactions—and the pools know it. If you will look at a newspaper giving the high and low prices of all stocks on the New York Stock Exchange for an entire year, you may observe a surprising number of stocks whose high for the year was a figure ending in a 4 or a 9, or, in other words, just under a multiple of five. Stocks make a high price of 124 or 149 far oftener than they reach 125 or 150. The reason is that we think in round numbers and try to sell at a round number but don't always succeed.

Imagine a room with buyers on one side and sellers on the other side. The majority of sellers are asking, let us suppose, 150 for a stock, but the best bid is only 149. Finally, enough sellers decide to take 149 to fill at least part of the demand. Then the price drops to 148 and lower. All who held out for 150 now wish they had accepted 149. Pool managers are clever enough not to wait for round numbers but to sell ahead of the price asked by others.

Nearly always when a stock sells at 100 for the first time, it immediately goes still higher, because considerable pressure was required to push it to 100 and this same force is likely to carry it a little farther.

Reversing the process, the low price of your favorite stock for the year is fairly likely to be just above a five or a zero. More stocks sell down to 91 or 101 than to 90 or 100. We say of a favorite stock: "If it goes back to 90 I'm going to buy it."

But more experienced buyers may get in ahead by bidding 90½ or 91.

Inasmuch as a pool manager endeavors to sell stocks to the public at a price level not likely to be long maintained, he knows the buyers are going to lose money at least temporarily. Hence one might be justified in the assumption that a professional pool operator must necessarily be either unscrupulous or else so hardened to what he is doing that he has lost all sense of human sympathy. Now, if you had a neighbor who engaged in the grocery business and constantly sought to unload goods which would disappoint customers and cost them serious loss, you would probably hold such a fellow in contempt. He would have a hard time staying in business. But the pool doesn't deal directly with its customers and doesn't even know who they are; its ethical standards seem more impersonal and less cruel. The truth is that every one of us who fools with the market tries to carry out the same technique employed by the pools—to buy cheaply and sell dear. And we do this with no thought of unfair tactics, with no intention of harming any one to whom even a small loss may mean real hardship. As a matter of fact, the pool knows, as we all know, that the Wall Street game should be played only by those who can *afford* to lose. Those of us to whom a loss of a few hundred dollars is really vital haven't any business to be in the stock market at all.

Moreover, to give the devil his due, many pool operations probably have a benign influence, for they help to keep prices steady. Many of the most riotous and most dangerous advances in stock prices are made, not when a pool is operating, but when the uninformed public gets excited and bids up a stock, thinking not of its value, but only that it may sell still higher tomorrow. When realization suddenly comes that a price is too high, then a drop of 20 or 30 points may occur in a single day. The pools often get the blame when the real fault is the greediness of the public.

CHAPTER VII

WIN BY BEING CONTRARY!

Since, as we have seen, the natural behavior of the average person is likely to be wrong, and powerful interests are constantly at work to lure one into acting unwisely, what is one to do?

Fortunately, as already suggested, there is one fairly safe guide to prudent procedure—to do exactly the opposite from what the majority of other people are doing. If one would win he must be contrary.

Most people buy the wrong stocks, at the wrong time, sell at the wrong time and then pay the broker a handsome fee for executing these misguided orders.

Every successful speculator knows, and every keen student of human psychology knows, that the mass of people are overwhelmingly less intelligent than the few. All scientific intelligence tests, in the army, in schools and colleges, everywhere, indicate that about two per cent of all the people in any community are more capable of reaching logical conclusions than are the other 98 per cent. One may easily prove this simply by checking over his own list of acquaintances. You probably know at least one hundred persons fairly well. You may know several hundred; but of this list, you naturally know one hundred better than the others. Now, of this one hundred intimate friends, neighbors and other acquaintances, aren't there two or three who have far more sense, whose judgment on almost anything you would rather trust, than all the rest put together? It is probably safe to say that Henry Ford's judgment about the automobile business is usually more worth having than the composite opinion of all his thousands of employees. No matter how many people you start running around a race track, they can't overtake a champion, can they?

Surely it is reasonable to assume that the stock market has lured in a fairly representative cross-section of the public and that, therefore, if the majority of all people are less capable than the few of deciding anything sensibly, this must hold true likewise of their behavior in stocks. Indeed, it is even more true of people in the market, because of highly and skillfully organized plans to lead them astray. The game is always rigged by the smart to outwit the stupid.

To succeed in the market, then, one must not do what most others are doing. Hence it is dangerous to pay the slightest heed to what you most often hear or see—*vox populi, vox Dei,* regardless. But since most people are fairly sure to be wrong, he who does the opposite has a good chance to be right. We may not know what the highly intelligent minority are doing, but by watching and studying the crowd, we can pick up useful clues as to what that same minority are *not* doing. In other words, those of us who are only moderately intelligent and might not behave wisely by independent effort always have the opportunity to join up with smart folk if we'll just consistently pay no attention to all the signs which say: Follow the Crowd!

At this point, I am interrupted, maybe, by somebody who exclaims: "Hey, there! What you say is contrary to the whole spirit of democracy. We live under a system of majority rule and yet you say the majority is always wrong."

Yes, I feel sure that the majority is likely to be wrong except when following the leadership of a small, somewhat more intelligent, minority. The advantage of democracy isn't so much that people may act intelligently as that they have fair play—a chance to express themselves and get what they think they want.

The only trouble with this formula of doing the opposite from the crowd is that one isn't always sure what the crowd really is doing and anyhow it is not so easy as it sounds to go in the other direction even if one does know. When all our neighbors, our favorite financial pages and all other agencies keep drumming it into us that one line of action is wisdom, such thoughts become so merged with our own, if we ever had any of our own, that the line of least resistance is to do what everybody says. Even a high degree of intelligence won't always save you from doing wrong, unless you are mentally guyed and braced and on the alert against following the current.

The idea of making money by coppering the bets of the crowd, is not, however, a mere theory, for, as noted in a previous chapter, it is exactly what successful operators do. Men of wealth and power who have enough important contact with banks and other sources of information to know what is going on backstage, are able to tell when any stock or any group of stocks are overbought. When the public is too deeply in the market, on margin accounts, these big operators know that the market is top-heavy. They say the technical position is poor. It is just the time for them to sell. They even sell stocks that they don't own—that is, sell short, for they know that prices must go down.

Before the Big Crash of October 1929 the public had ample warning that the big fellows were selling and the little fellows buying. Week after week, the published report of the Federal Reserve Banks indicated that brokers' loans were going up, even though average stock prices were declining. In other words, the growth in loans could not be explained by greater value of stocks, for the price trend was downward. The figures could only indicate that the number of margin accounts—stocks held by brokers for customers, with loans against them—were increasing, while wiser folk, able to own their stocks outright, were selling. The only reason they could be selling was because, from their superior vantage point, they foresaw a decline and expected to repurchase their stocks at lower levels. Nobody could have asked for a better hint to step out of the market. The danger signal was adequate and unmistakable. But how many of us heeded it?

Surely Wall Street's gigantic Hallowe'en festival provided an overwhelming variety of proof that most people are always wrong. Otherwise the vast majority would not have deliberately placed themselves in a situation where they could be compelled to dump good stocks at hysterically low prices for the benefit of the wiser few. No great feat of logical reasoning was needed to arrive at the conclusion that all these people had been wrong or imprudent even before the catastrophe occurred. When you note that a stock sold for $1 a share when the current quarterly earnings of that same stock are $1.50, you know that somebody has not behaved as a Napoleon of finance. Yet thousands of persons were almost equally foolish.

Wise men—wise, that is, so far as the stock market is concerned—had been selling their stocks at the very time that the general public was most eager to buy. Indeed, the readiness of the public to buy was what gave the cagey ones a beautiful opportunity to sell. One of the reasons for the stupendous size of the selling panic was probably this: When the first warning break came, early in October, the public, instead of selling, mistook the slightly lower prices for bargains and used cash reserves to buy still more stocks. Naturally this added to the burden of protecting their holdings as prices receded and the largest group sold—or were sold out—when most prices reached their exact bottom. As prices went lower, the volume and speed of sales increased! But how many people, aside from the Morgans and the Rockefellers, bought at these incredibly low prices? Bargains that you wouldn't have believed if you hadn't seen them were available all over the list, but none of us wanted them, even if we still had money left, because we reasoned: Stocks are in a violent downward trend; therefore, they'll go still lower tomorrow! Whatever *is* will always continue!

I'm reminded of the remark of a famous speculator, who after making—and keeping—a big fortune in Wall Street, remarked: "I have done only what other people wanted me to. When they were determined to sell their stocks in a falling market at whatever prices they could get and clamored for buyers, I accommodated them by buying. When they were equally anxious to buy stocks at high prices, I agreeably permitted them to buy mine."

If you were to go into a broker's board room during a wave of panicky selling and bargain prices, you might observe that though everybody who is trading at all is selling, not a soul is buying. Obviously, *somebody* must be buying, or else there couldn't be any market. Who is buying when everybody in sight is selling? This much is certain: the buyer, whoever and wherever he is, is some one too shrewd, whose time is too valuable, to be sitting about watching price changes on a big blackboard. A man important enough to be in big league affairs can't possibly spare more than a few minutes once or twice a year in his broker's office.

Even that part of the uninformed public which somehow had not been in the market during the 1929 slaughter, and so still had money, did not begin to buy until after they had seen stocks rebound. The bulk of buying, by people who took their money out of building and loan companies and savings banks to pick up supposed bargains, did not come until after most stocks had regained half of their losses. Hosts of persons who had been frightened into selling at the bottom decided that the trend had changed and bought back the same identical stocks at prices 25 or 30 points higher. If you think this is exaggerated, ask any broker.

Now it must be obvious that if a person had taken a few thousand dollars of capital and, beginning early in October, sold stocks every time the majority bought, and bought them only when nearly everybody else was selling, he could have made a comfortable fortune, all within one month.

It is not always possible to do so well so quickly by going contrary to the majority, but I'm convinced that the secret of success in the stock market lies in adopting that formula for most of the time.

Another reason for behaving differently from the majority is that the human mind is inclined to go back to the last experience in the market and judge the future by that.

Most people look back rather than forward. In 1922 and 1923, tremendous profits were made (by those smart enough to sell at the right time) in the Standard Oil stocks. Wise men tell us now that John D. Rockefeller and his associates, who foresaw that the oil industry would have a few rough years, were selling many of their oil shares in 1922 and 1923. The favorable market for their selling may have been manufactured for their purposes, or maybe it just happened to come their way. At any rate, it is now evident that there was much inside selling. Records show that for many of the Standard Oil issues, the best return in earnings came in 1919 and 1920. But the speculative fireworks in such stocks did not come until two or three years later? Why? Because, in order to sell out, when they saw that the best was over for a few years, insiders had to dress up these stocks and make them spectacular to appeal to people who thought that increasing earnings and increasing values would go on forever. As part of this plan of insiders to sell to the public, big pools were formed, stock dividends provided in great profusion—and, sure enough, the public bought crazily. While insiders were unloading, clever professional short-term speculators also were able to make immense profits.

But right at the time when the shrewd ones were getting out, in 1923, the rank and file of long-term investors were hopelessly hooked in such stocks as Standard Oil of New Jersey, bought at, say, 49. They had to hold the stock for several years without much profit and without large dividends. During the 1929 crash, when newspapers were carrying large headlines about John D. Rockefeller trying to buy a vast block of Standard of New Jersey at 50, one couldn't help thinking how wise old John D. had doubtless been to keep his money in more productive lines for five or six years and let the public patiently hold his stocks until he got good and ready to take them back at bargain prices.

The point to all this, I repeat, is that the public looks back when it should look forward. The average speculator thinks that the stocks which went up in the last bull market are the ones most likely to go up in the next one. Hence, one must steer clear of mere average judgment.

In 1923, after the distribution of oil stocks had been accomplished, prices of these stocks naturally began to sag. They reached even lower levels in the fall than in the summer. In December of that year, however, and in January and February of 1924, speculation in the oil group was revived, largely because of the efforts of one big operator who still had more stock to be distributed. Again the public bought heavily. People were easily induced to buy because they remembered how profitable oils had been in the previous bull market. Everybody figured that since oils had been the leaders in one bull market, it naturally followed that they would once more be the bellwether of the next bull market. Such reasoning! The truth was that on February 8, 1924, the Standard Oil stocks made their high for five years, just three months away from the greatest bull market in history. When these stocks were declining in 1924, everybody said:

"Buy Standard Oil stocks. Safest investments in the world. Nobody ever lost a dollar buying this group. Don't buy motors. Too speculative. Look at what happened to General Motors in 1920 and 1921"—and much more similar rubbish.

When a great majority of people believe that everything is perfectly safe and that nothing can happen, we are quite likely to have a panic—because that is the very time that stocks are most easily passed from strong hands into weak hands. When the majority of people are cautious and buy only a little, we usually have a rising market. We nearly always have the greatest public short interest just prior to a market advance—since the short interest helps to start the advance—and the smallest short interest right before a decline, as happened in the fall of 1929. When speculators have been well educated, as they were in 1929, to buy stocks on any decline, distribution can be accomplished on the way down with considerable ease.

The education which made this possible had been done partly by a series of important episodes. After the moderate smash of December 1928, the public refused to buy heavily, because of a belief that money rates might be higher in January. Again, in March 1929, when money rates soared to 20 per cent, everybody looked for a panic after stocks broke, and refused to buy. When the Federal Reserve discount rate was raised, in the summer of 1929 to 6 per cent, everybody said: "Now the panic surely will come." But two days later stocks started once more rapidly upward. By September, when everybody was thoroughly convinced that nothing could happen, Mr. Babson, who has often been decidedly wrong, predicted a panic; but that only fanned the flames of bullish buying enthusiasm—for everybody had seen what looked like ample proof that nothing could happen now. Hadn't the Federal Reserve played its last trump card—with failure? Indeed, by September, that board had itself probably given up all hope of curbing the market—and that fact itself to really wise speculators was the greatest danger signal of all. Some nine months of education had been required to place the public in this frame of mind that nothing could happen. But now the harvest season was at hand. Feeling sure that a decline was simply an opportunity to buy stocks, the public would gladly buy on the way down. So much for the human habit of looking back when it should look ahead. And the human mind is the one element in speculation that is always fixed and will never change.

We have already seen that charts and other mechanical means for beating the market are not dependable, for chart-readers are easily fooled. To understand the market, one must think of the human element—of the great mass of unthinking speculators and investors who are going to be wrong. No two speculative moves are ever the same; no two markets are ever alike; and no two market manipulators ever operate alike. It is like a bridge game in which the same combination of cards may never occur again in your lifetime. But if you play carefully and watch each move of the other fellow, you nevertheless have a chance to come out ahead in the long run.

You can't beat the stock market, we are assured, any

more than you can hold back the tides. But why try to hold back the tides or to overcome an irresistible force of any kind? Instead of trying to pick a fuss with the tides, why not ride *with* them? In other words, as a politician once said to me: "If you can't lick an organization, join it!"

The stock market moves up and down in great waves. Most people, being less smart than a few people, invariably mistake the trend of these waves and therefore buy and sell stocks at the wrong time. To get aboard the tide at the right time, it is only necessary to disagree with the opinion of most of your neighbors who are following what they consider logical reasoning processes.

Be contrary! But be cautious!

Chapter VIII

About Watching One's Step

Disrelishing toil as I do, I have an idea that I shall play the stock market as long as I live. While it will never be my main occupation, I believe that by occasionally buying stocks when they are under-priced and selling them when they are over-priced, I may contrive to minimize arduous work at my regular trade as a writing man. It isn't that I enjoy playing the market. I don't enjoy it. And I have no gambling instincts. I have never seen a horse-race in my life, let alone bet on one, dislike card-playing, crap-shooting and all games of chance. But the market seems to provide an easier means than is otherwise available to gain the price of leisure to travel, and do all the other things that I really wish to do. I have no intention of ever plunging or gambling in stocks, or of risking my birthplace for a mess of potash, as O. Henry might say; but when opportunity knocks I shall go to the door and see what's up. Above all, though, I shall be careful—oh, how careful! I shall always follow the hypothesis that it's more important to avoid losing than to win. Losses hurt one's morale. When thinking of buying a stock expected to rise, I shall first of all ascertain if its earnings and outlook make it reasonably loss-proof.

While I have frequently carried margin accounts with from one to three brokers, I am strongly of the opinion that I shall make more money if I buy only as much stock as I can pay cash for and not carry any on margin. Then there will be no need of becoming alarmed and selling too soon, or of buying too much and being *compelled* to sell at the wrong time. If one buys good stocks and the old U.S.A. prospers, he will make a profit; but if he buys all that he can on margin, then he may lose, no matter how prosperous the country is, or how good the stock.[1]

With a good stock owned outright, one can afford to wait a long time if need be, for an expected rise. (Since money left in the bank draws interest at only four per cent, why complain if one must wait a year or two for a stock to appreciate 50 per cent?) The margin player must have the wisdom not only to select a good stock that will eventually have a decided price advance, but he must pick it at a time when it will not go much lower even temporarily.

Another objection to margin accounts is that they create a psychological handicap even when stocks never go below one's original purchase price. When on margin, you are in the hands of your creditors and this is not a happy situation. Hence you are likely to exhaust your store of patience needlessly soon and sell out long before a stock has done all

---

[1]We are sometimes inclined to buy on margin because the little we can buy outright seems too trivial. Unable to deal in stocks on a grand scale ourselves, we feel woefully picayunish as we see transactions of thousands of shares passing on the tape. Yet the truth is that one doesn't need to have many hundreds of shares to control more than an average person in the market does. After talking with about twenty-five margin clerks in leading brokerage houses, as well as with many members of such firms, I am convinced that an average margin account, even with the market booming, is not more than two hundred shares. Yet the aggregate of such modest accounts is of real consequence. One-fourth of all the common stock of the great United States Steel Corporation, for example, is usually held on margin. We small traders are not so small after all.

Moreover, we small investors, plain folk who have saved a little money but must work and struggle for most of our income, are the real owners of this country's industries. Great railroad systems do not belong to bankers who wear side-whiskers and live in palatial homes full of haughty servants, but to ordinary people who drive inexpensive little cars and occupy modest little houses or apartments.

The average stockholder of the New York Central Railroad owns only about 60 shares. More than half of the American Telegraph and Telephone Company belongs to people who have less than ten shares apiece. Everywhere the big wealthy corporations are being spread around, owned more and more not by the few but by the many.

that it might. Several years ago, I bought five hundred shares of the old General Motors stock, on margin, at 57. Some months later I sold out at a substantial profit; but I should have made far more by buying only 100, or even 50 shares, outright, and waiting at least three years before selling. How many men could sit patiently for three years to sell a stock held on margin?

Owning stocks outright, however, is by no means sure protection against loss in the market. If you pay $10,000 for shares that decline to a value of only $3,000, you have taken a terrible loss, and may continue to have that loss for several years, even though you're not compelled to sell. Many people suffered big losses in the panic of 1929 mainly because they had their stocks well margined, or fully paid for, and were thus able to hang on too long. They would have lost less money if wiped out on the first dip. When you have so much money in the broker's hands that you are immune to margin calls, it doesn't follow that you aren't quietly taking a terrible licking.

We often hear this stock or that recommended as one "to put away in your box and forget." But no stock should ever be considered that safe. New inventions, changes in industry, are constantly making certain lines of goods obsolete and bringing others to the fore. Twenty years ago, one-fourth of all goods sold by the biggest hardware company in the United States had something to do with a horse, buggy or wagon. But how would you like to have remained these twenty years a heavy stockholder in a buggy-whip corporation? Years ago, canal stocks were among the most conservative of investments, suitable for widows and orphans—much as the more gilt-edged railroad shares are today. Most people who owned canal stocks put them away and forgot about them. But it was a strange fact that these canal stocks reached the highest prices in their history—presumably through clever propaganda and manipulation—shortly before they started a descent that continued all the way to zero! Investors who held canal stocks might better have had them on margin and been forced to examine their value sooner.

Whether buying on margin or outright, *one should determine at the time of a stock purchase, just how much money
he is willing to lose* on that particular stock before he will
believe that it isn't as good as he was led to think. Having
decided to limit your loss at a definite point in an emer-
gency, then you are just as safe on margin as owning outright—and possibly even safer.

Looking back on several years' experience, I know that
every time my broker ever asked me for margin, *I should
have refused to give it to him.* Instead, I should have sold
enough stock to bring my account down to his require-
ments. The fact that he had what he had thought, and what
I had thought, was enough margin, and we find that we
both were mistaken, should be enough to indicate that
something unexpectedly unfavorable has happened, and it
is no time to be putting more money into the market. If
unwilling to sell stocks when the broker wants more margin, then one should dig up enough money to pay for the
stocks outright. Otherwise, the only result of adding more
margin money may be to lose that also.

Though I expect to buy stocks from time to time, when I
think they are under-priced, and sell them when they have
reached their full value, I don't recommend that my friends
do the same thing. I'm convinced that many a highly intelligent person has no business dabbling with stocks at all,
because too handicapped by temperament not suited to this
particular game. To begin with, the stock market is no place
for a person who lets strong convictions take root in his
mind and stay there. The man who is a Republican, or a
Baptist, simply because his father was and he was brought
up that way, will find a better haven for his talents elsewhere. Conditions sometimes shift so rapidly that one not
only shouldn't do what he was planning five minutes previous, but should do the exact opposite. Instead of selling all
you have, perhaps you should suddenly turn optimistic and
buy. The average person when reminded of having changed
his mind about a long-cherished opinion is usually more
apologetic than flattered. Obstinacy may have its place

among the virtues, but a mind where beliefs crystallize and won't be dislodged is not ideal for successful operations in Wall Street.

Not only should a speculator avoid holding too fast to his opinions, but he must be disinclined to look backward. Otherwise, he will be perpetually unhappy. No one has ever yet made a perfect speculative operation. If you buy at the exact bottom and sell at the exact top, then you are disgusted with yourself because you didn't have more faith in your judgment and buy more. Any one temperamentally inclined to look back or hold post-mortem examinations should let stocks alone.

Another group, and it is a large group, who should stay away from Wall Street, is made up of those who expect the good things of life to come too easily and therefore are unwilling to put forth proper effort to find out which stocks are good. Only a few of us are naturally so lazy that we are willing to study and work desperately hard at times, in the hope of working less hard later on. I have often gone on a long railroad journey to investigate a corporation whose stock I am thinking of buying. Anybody with a reporter's instincts, and plenty of curiosity, can keep asking questions until he satisfies himself that a thing is good, or not quite so good. But most people are not willing to go to all this bother and prefer simply to accept the advice of the stranger sitting alongside of them in a broker's office. Indeed, I know of only one kind of commitment that people make with less investigation than when they buy stocks, and that is when they get married. A man who would spend an hour shopping for a shirt, may select a stock or a wife after only the most casual inquiry. Likewise, the same person who would seek expert advice before investing $10,000 in a home, will invest that much in the stock of an unknown corporation as readily as he would buy a collar button. The type of person who is bored with the idea of having to look before he leaps should let the stock market stay right where it is.

Because many intelligent people are certain to lose in

speculation, and even in investments, it is a grave question whether thrift itself is equally wise for all kinds of folk. Why battle to save money if the Wall Street boys are going to take it from you? Not long ago, a woman asked me how to go about saving and investing money to give her independence in old age. I found that by stinting herself over a period of years, she might be able to save about $5,000 before the age of 55. This at six per cent would give her only $25 a month, which wouldn't be enough to keep her. I therefore recommended that she not try to save much money but buy rouge and pretty clothes and make herself so charming that some Adonis of wealth and station will be sure to marry her and then she won't need to worry. I still think that the advice, for her case at least, was fairly good.

An acquaintance of mine lost his entire fortune, about $71,000, in the October '29 smash—all but $800. After many sleepless nights, he was in such serious nervous condition that his physician ordered a trip to Lake Placid for a complete rest. I met him and his wife as they were starting for the train.

"We have been planning a trip together for years, a sort of second honeymoon," he told me, with a brave smile, "but we never felt that we could afford it *until now*."

Sensible expenditure for something that one greatly desires is often the best way to make paper profits real. I long ago made this rule for myself: When I have a profit and there is something that I would greatly like to buy, I dispose of stocks and buy it, even though it looks as if I might make still more by waiting. Several times I have taken profits for a trip to Europe when I had to think regretfully of the additional advance my stocks might have made. But every time, without exception, the stocks I sold for such a trip later went much lower rather than higher. And, oh, boy, when you are bowling along amidst gorgeous European scenery, all expenses paid by Wall Street, and you note a decline in value of stocks you sold, how nice it is to sit back and think that you're getting something nobody can take away from you!

The advantage of selling stocks in which you have profits to buy something you want, or that your family wants, is not only that you make temporary profits permanent, but you have an opportunity to view the market from a different seat out in the audience. Maybe you were reluctant to sell certain stocks that had always been good friends to you; but, having sold, do you feel like buying those same stocks back? It often makes a tremendous difference which side of the fence you're on, and there's nothing like an unprejudiced view from the sidelines to help you to act with sanity. I know a young man connected with an investment trust who went for six months, a while ago, predicting practically every up and down move in stocks, almost to the hour. Anybody who followed his predictions could have made money. Yet he himself carried no stocks during that time, and that was why his predictions were so good. When he does operate in the market he is only moderately successful; because, when trading, he goes according to his prejudices instead of being free and unbiased to face facts.

The most dangerous thing that can happen to one splashing into the market and getting his feet wet for the first time, is to be too successful right off. Since most of us want something for nothing, and secretly expect something for nothing, quick profits only help to confirm one's belief that they will come easily. Two or three lucky experiences and a person is ready to risk his all. I know a young clerical worker who scraped together $1,000 and arranged to open a marginal account with a broker. One morning he telephoned to inquire about prices and said:

"I'd buy one hundred shares of General Universal if I had time to bring you over a check. But I'll wait until tomorrow."

"You don't need to wait," replied the broker affably. "We know you have the money ready and you can buy the stock now if you wish to."

That was at eleven o'clock in the morning. Three hours later he sold out at a profit of $480! Mind you, he hadn't yet had time to put up a cent of money. He just walked over the next day and received the broker's check for $480 representing the happy difference between his buying and selling price on one hundred shares.

Small wonder if his regular job, with a modest weekly wage, began to look downright ridiculous. He soon felt such confidence in himself that at the end of five weeks his profits, along with his original $1,000, were all gone.

More painful, but far safer in the long run, was the experience of another young man I know who used Scotch caution in his first market transaction. "I want to buy a hundred shares of United States Steel if it goes down to 175," he told his broker, "but I don't want to let the market ever go far against me, so as soon as you have bought it, put a stop loss order to sell if it drops to 172."

Half an hour later, the broker phoned to the young man to announce that he had executed *both orders!* Steel had dipped down to 172—and then started back up again—and the young trading novitiate was out $300, besides the broker's commission. Swift and sad, but a valuable lesson. He eventually made a little money.

A surprisingly large number of speculators make up what Colonel Ayres calls the lunatic fringe. They are not only in the market over their heads, but are willing to risk money that they could never replace. When a man with earning power of less than $5,000 a year has an inheritance of, say, $50,000 up on margin, he can only be regarded as at least temporarily insane. He not only shouldn't risk his entire fortune on margin, but shouldn't have it in stocks at all. Not less than half of it should be permanently invested in high-grade bonds. Personally, I find it a good rule never to risk in the stock market more than could be replaced, if the worst happened, by strict economy, over a period of one year.

Many a man or woman who would not expect to be successful as a circus clown, opera singer, or grocer, without some kind of preparation or talent, nevertheless expects to be successful right off in the stock market—probably the most intricate and difficult game on earth. The reason for this faith in success without any special qualification is doubtless the almost universal belief in luck. Except for the widespread belief in luck, perhaps the stock market could hardly keep going on its present scale. But, somebody says, intelligent people don't believe in luck. Ah, but they do! No matter how intelligent you may be, you have a sneaking faith in the back of your head that some special attribute in yourself will somehow protect you from misfortune. When you hear of a bad railroad accident, you can't picture yourself as being on a train at such a time. You say to yourself: "That would never happen to me." When the insurance company tells you that your life expectancy is a certain number of years, you secretly expect to live considerably longer than that, because of your belief that you yourself are especially blessed. Everybody is like that. You see a bunch of gamins playing craps. One of them has gradually lost until his last penny is gone. He turns to a pal and asks: "Lend me a quarter, will you?"—sure that if he just had a little more money, he could win back all he lost. Likewise, the man who, through lack of the right kind of preparation or temperament, has persistently lost in the market for ten years keeps right on playing, with unfaltering faith in his ultimate success. His record strongly indicates that he is not qualified for the thing he is trying to do, but he never loses his belief in his own ultimate good luck.

On the other hand, now that we have pointed out dangers of speculation, it is only fair to say that it is also possible to exaggerate the hazards. It is just as foolish to think that everybody who buys a few shares of common stocks is going to lose heavily as to think that any one who samples a glass of home brew is doomed to fill a drunkard's grave.

Indeed, nearly everybody is more or less a speculator. The corner grocer speculates when he buys potatoes at wholesale prices expecting to sell them at a profit. Even "short sales" are more common in everyday life than is ordinarily believed. When a contractor agrees to build a house at a certain price, he intends to buy the material when he needs it. Thus he has sold something that he didn't yet own, in the belief that he can "cover," that is, buy the material when the time comes, at a price that will permit a profit.

What makes it comparatively safe to buy carefully selected common stocks for investment is the fact that the population of the world keeps growing and the demand for most good products is always increasing. We have become a nation of investors and stock gamblers mostly since our entry into the World War and perhaps the foundation for our interest in the fluctuating prices of securities was laid by the four-minute men, during the war, when they induced us to buy Liberty bonds. Many of us never before had known the satisfaction of going to a wee safety-deposit box and clipping a coupon.

Having hit on this improved method of saving money, we carried the idea still further and bought other bonds—not only Liberty bonds, but municipal and industrial bonds. But our financial education was just starting.

Now that we had learned to buy bonds, we began to think about stocks too, and not only gilt-edged preferred stocks, suitable for widow and orphans, but common stocks. Interest in common stocks was greatly boosted by the publication of a book by Edgar L. Smith, dealing with Common Stocks As Long Term Investments.

The story is that Smith was employed by a bond house to make a far-reaching investigation and then write a report to prove the advantages of bonds over all other forms of securities for long-time investments. But as he dug deeper and deeper into the facts, he found that he must prove what he hadn't intended—that the most profitable investments are a diversified list of good dividend-paying common stocks.

The point is that we are an industrial nation and our successful industries keep growing. You buy a $1,000 bond at par and when it is due in twenty or thirty years, you get $1,000 back again; but perhaps the $1,000 you now receive is not as valuable as the $1,000 you paid in the first place, because it won't buy as much. The purchasing power of the dollar may have been shrinking gradually during the intervening years, in which event you actually have lost money.

On the other hand, if you bought common stock which

gave you not only a dividend claim but real ownership of part of a growing company in an expanding industry, then your stock became more and more valuable in proportion to the success of the company.

When we read in the newspapers the list of securities held by a multimillionaire when he dies and his will is filed, we can't help being impressed by the fact that these shrewd, rich old fellows seem to have had a great liking for common stocks. They didn't get rich merely by going to the bank every Saturday with part of their earnings; they planted their money where it would take root, branch and grow.

On top of the newly aroused interest in owning securities came a long, uninterrupted period of exceptional prosperity. The rise in prices of many stocks was justified by increasing earnings. These earnings have been possible because you and I have been drawing good wages and could buy the articles that the big companies have to sell. Great corporations are prosperous because we are.

With stocks available in hundreds of well-managed, expanding enterprises, it seems as if making money in the market should be almost as easy as losing. Indeed, profits *would* be easy enough, except for the great obstacle of human nature. Here we are in the foremost industrial nation on earth, literally surrounded by companies bound to grow and become more valuable. But what good is such an opportunity in the face of impatience, greed, vanity and all the other little human quirks which make us behave foolishly? What does it avail us to buy into a company with a marvellous future, if we become discouraged after a few weeks and sell our interest, during a period of temporary dullness, just because of pessimistic gossip in the papers?

I can offer a rule for successful market operations—anybody can make such a rule—that would be almost sure-fire, if one were to adopt it and stick to it. The rule might be worded something like this:

Buy stocks of companies that have shown gradually increasing earnings in essential industries, that is, industries making articles that people can't well do without; but don't buy, no matter how good the stocks are, until the whole market has definitely *quit going down on bad news;* then *sell all your stocks when the market has ceased to advance on good news.*

That simple rule, with a little additional qualifying, would surely make money for anybody who followed it. But try to do it! Unless you are a genius—and frankly, reader, I gravely doubt if you are—you will make your share of blunders, just as most of us do, and then at the end of a period of rising prices, you will wonder how you could have failed to make more money during such a favorable time. If you are just an average person, which is altogether probable, you will not have the patience to make a careful enough investigation of a stock before buying; or even if you do that, you will not have patience to wait until the market has shown definite resistance to bad news. But if you should somehow avoid these errors, then your greed will force you to wait too long to sell, and your paper profits will melt away.

I asked a friend, a keen student of the market, and a successful speculator, to tell me just how he goes about making profitable commitments in stocks.

"The first thought," he replied, "should be to try to ascertain the trend of the market. That should govern seven out of ten votes on the question of staying out of the market or stepping in. The next two votes should be on the *industry* you are going to select, and the last vote on the particular stock. Fundamental statistics and economics are helpful, if correct—but the big danger is that they may not be correct. Suppose that the best analysis of the situation you could make, some weeks after the Big Crash, leads you to believe that we are going to have a few weeks or months of rising market. Then you should buy rather than sell and not be short of a single share—for if you are short, you are not only fighting one stock but the whole market trend. Next, you study various industries and find, say, that the motion picture group will have big earnings reported in the following six months. Then, let us suppose, you find that this group of stocks have not discounted their favorable situation, with ratio of prices and earnings more attractive than ever before. We are justified in assuming that slow accumulation may be going on in this group, but that the general public is probably staying out, because of uncertainty inspired by the credit difficulties of William Fox. It is almost inconceivable that the public would buy on a large scale in the amusement stocks just yet, but quite likely, on the other hand, that a large short interest may be developing. The chances are that if one stock in this group shows signs of trying to creep higher, the impetus must be quiet buying by insiders.

"The best way to tell what the market is going to do is to talk with as many amateur traders as possible. If they are courageously short of stocks, I know that hundreds, perhaps thousands, more are also on the short side, and I am therefore inclined to be bullish for a healthy upward swing. If the public is timidly bearish, then I expect only a minor bulge."

We not only have statistical evidence that the majority have always been led by human impulses to make wrong moves, and to lose money, but it is a simple process of reasoning to prove that the majority of us *must* always be wrong in the market and are certain to lose. To begin with, we know that to gain profit one must buy when prices are comparatively low and sell when prices are higher. But if most people had the foresight to take advantage of low prices and buy, then the low prices wouldn't exist since there would then be more buyers than sellers. Likewise, if the majority of us were cagey enough to sell the instant that stocks are priced beyond their worth, then peak prices would never be reached. In short, if everybody were truly intelligent, no one would sell too cheaply or pay too much, and the result would be that the wide swings in prices could not occur. Price ranges would be confined to such narrow limits that no speculator would pay much attention to the market. There wouldn't be a market! Speculation can be worth while only when a few are taking advantage of the stupidity of the many.[1]

A moment's thought will show that important episodes in the market cannot possibly occur when everybody thinks they will. If, following a panic, nearly everybody decides that the market will be in a gradual decline until the middle of April, then without the shadow of a doubt the bottom of the decline will come either earlier or later than the middle of April; for, those who expect stocks to hit their lows in April will naturally sell their holdings sooner, with the intention of buying them back when they are at the bottom. This selling, in anticipation of bottom prices later on, would probably be the very cause of forcing stocks to their final lows much sooner than generally expected. Likewise, if everybody believes that the top of the market will come in October, they will sell in August or September, and then there wouldn't be any top in October.

Whether your operations are large or small, your only chance to take money from Wall Street is to be somewhat

---

[1]Come to think of it, a big drop in the price of a company's stock doesn't really represent a decrease in the value of that company, because no considerable amount of the stock could ever have sold at the top price, and therefore that price never represented true value. Suppose you are a big stockholder, owning, say, 100,000 shares, in a company with a total of 500,000 shares of common stock outstanding. You note by the papers that the price of this stock has advanced from its original $2 a share to $10 a share. This, you reflect, maks your holdings worth $1,000,000. But you couldn't get that much, for if you tried to sell your 100,000 shares, you would break the price. The only way you could get $10 a share would be through pool activity and propaganda to force the price much higher before you start to unload. When United States Steel common was selling around 262, one might have multiplied that price by the number of shares in existence and offered the resulting figure as the worth of the United States Steel Corporation. But this would have been a fallacious value, since there was no possible way for all the stock, or even a substantial fraction of the stock, to be sold at that price.

In certain respects then a person who plays the market in a small way has great advantages over a big operator. Granted that he has equal intelligence and skill, he can make more money, for the amount used, than if his transactions were on a grand scale—for he can buy low and sell high without disturbing the market.

unusual. Since the majority must be wrong, success can come only from doing the opposite from what the crowd is doing. There is no possible way by which everybody can stand at the same place at the same time. But what makes it difficult to go contrary to the crowd is the skill of big interests in misleading all the players who make up the rank and file. Each of us thinks to himself: "Everybody is doubtless doing that; so I'll do the opposite!" But, you see, with each of us confidently feeling that he is being *different,* the result is simply that most of us behave just about alike.

We gradually learn some of the tricks that are used to fool us. But unless we watch our steps carefully, we don't learn soon enough—not until after our money is gone. *The game is old—but the players are always new!*

THE END